WALKS INTO HISTORY

CHESHIRE

Brian Conduit

COUNTRYSIDE BOOKS
NEWBURY BERKSHIRE

COUNTRYSIDE BOOKS
3 Catherine Road
Newbury, Berkshire

To view our complete range of books,
please visit us at
www.countrysidebooks.co.uk

ISBN 978 1 84674 072 5

Photographs by the author
Maps by Gelder Design & Mapping
Designed by Peter Davies, Nautilus Design

Produced through MRM Associates Ltd., Reading
Typeset by CJWT Solutions, St Helens
Printed in Thailand

*All material for the manufacture of this book
was sourced from sustainable forests.*

Contents

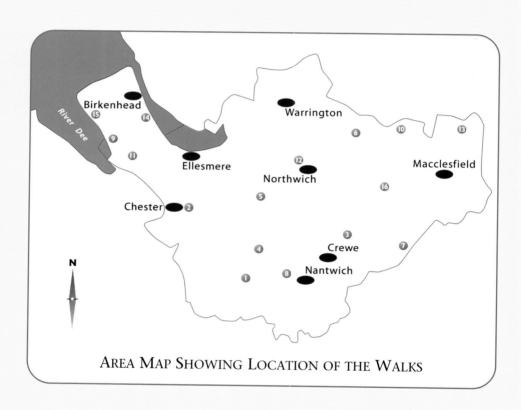

AREA MAP SHOWING LOCATION OF THE WALKS

PUBLISHER'S NOTE

We hope that you obtain considerable enjoyment from this book; great care has been taken in its preparation. Although at the time of publication all routes followed public rights of way or permitted paths, diversion orders can be made and permissions withdrawn.

We cannot, of course, be held responsible for such diversion orders and any inaccuracies in the text which result from these or any other changes to the routes nor any damage which might result from walkers trespassing on private property. We are anxious though that all details covering the walks are kept up to date and would therefore welcome information from readers which would be relevant to future editions.

The simple sketch maps that accompany the walks in this book are based on notes made by the author whilst checking out the routes on the ground. They are designed to show you how to reach the start, to point out the main features of the overall circuit and they contain a progression of numbers that relate to the paragraphs of the text.

However, for the benefit of a proper map, we do recommend that you purchase the relevant Ordnance Survey sheet covering your walk. The Ordnance Survey maps are widely available, especially through booksellers and local newsagents.

INTRODUCTION

Cheshire is a frontier county and not just in the obvious sense of sharing a border with Wales. In many ways it is a transitional zone between the north of England and the Midlands. Scenically the county has many facets. In the north-west is the Wirral peninsula between the Dee and Mersey, traditionally part of the county but now shared with Merseyside. The eastern edge of Cheshire forms part of the Peak District and has a decidedly Pennine flavour with mill towns and villages reminiscent of those further north in Lancashire and Yorkshire. To the south and south-west the county merges almost imperceptibly into its Staffordshire and Shropshire neighbours, with countryside more like that of the Midlands than the north.

The landscape most typical of Cheshire is of gently undulating terrain of lush pastures watered by slowly meandering rivers and dotted with small towns and pleasant villages that contain fine sandstone churches, black and white cottages and nice old pubs. This is dairy farming country where the traditional Cheshire cheese is produced. A distinctive feature is the well-wooded sandstone ridge that runs north to south across the middle of the county. From here stunning views stretch from the Dee and Mersey estuaries to Staffordshire and from the ridges of the Peak District to the hills of north Wales.

Scattered throughout this varied landscape are the many historic monuments that range chronologically from a prehistoric hillfort to the ultra-modern Jodrell Bank Observatory. As a frontier county, it is not surprising that defence is a recurring theme, starting with the scanty remains of the Roman legionary fort of Deva (Chester) and continuing with the medieval castles built to protect the Welsh border. Edward I's successful wars against the Welsh in the late 13th century and the subsequent incorporation of Wales into England led to more settled times. Farming prospered and from the later Middle Ages through to the Victorian era landowners erected the many timber-framed manor houses and later the grand stately homes for which Cheshire is particularly famed.

Although never a major industrial county, the Industrial Revolution made its mark on Cheshire – particularly in the north – where a number of textile mills were built. Possibly the greatest visual impact of the Industrial Revolution was the construction of the large number of canals that criss-cross the county, linking it with north Wales, the Midlands and the Mersey estuary. Nowadays these are mainly used for leisure and their towpaths make great walking routes.

Historic walks are fun and bring interest and variety to country walks by combining attractive countryside with places of historic significance. Cheshire has an abundance of both and, to add further interest, two urban routes have been included.

Brian Conduit

WALK 1
MAIDEN CASTLE AND PREHISTORIC HILLFORTS

Length: 4 miles

Bickerton Hill

HOW TO GET THERE: From the A534 turn along Hill Lane – this is nearly ½ mile to the west of the Copper Mine pub at Fuller's Moor – turn right along Hall Lane and at a T-junction turn left. Follow the lane for about ¾ mile and the car park is along an unmarked track on the left just before a lane on the right signposted to Tilston.

PARKING: Free National Trust car park at Bickerton Hill

MAP: OS Explorer 257 (Crewe & Nantwich) GR 494526

INTRODUCTION

Much of this walk is through the beautiful woodlands that clothe the slopes of the sandstone ridge in this part of south Cheshire. On the return leg over Bickerton Hill there is a series of superb viewpoints and the route passes through the earthworks of a prehistoric hillfort.

HISTORICAL BACKGROUND

Hillforts are found all over Britain and most of them were constructed during the Iron Age which lasted from around 800 BC to the arrival of the Romans in AD 43. They had a primarily defensive purpose and comprised earthen ramparts, often strengthened by timber and stone, within which there were various stone and timber structures.

These forts are the most numerous remaining structures of the Iron Age and

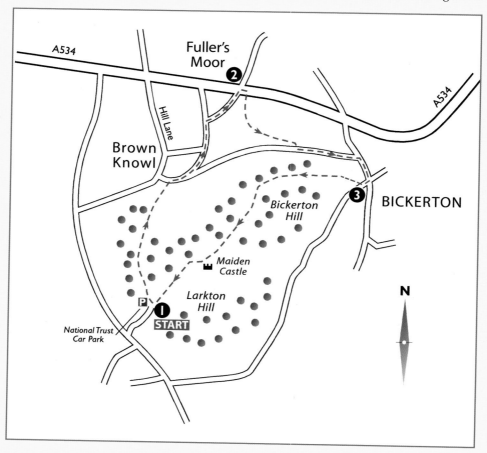

around 3000 examples have been recorded throughout Britain and Ireland. They varied considerably in size, ranging from simple small enclosures of under 1 acre to large and complex sites with two or more concentric ramparts covering over 200 acres. Although defensive and taking advantage of the natural steepness of the hills they occupied, they were civilian as well as military settlements and could be religious, administrative or commercial centres. The defences were to give them some protection from enemies and in this respect they can be seen as the predecessors of the walled towns of the Middle Ages.

Most seem to have been originally built between 750 and 500 BC but the reasons for this are not clear. Was the period between 750 and 500 BC a particularly troubled and warlike one? We do not know but there is evidence that there was widespread immigration at the time. One plausible explanation is that as this was a period of population growth which saw an expansion of more permanent farming methods, there was a need to protect tribal territories and for strong leaders to oversee this protection and exert more control over the population.

Although found all over the country, there are particularly heavy concentrations of hillforts in Wales, the Welsh Border area, south-west England and south-east Scotland. Again we are not sure why but can only assume that these areas, even at this early stage in our history, were unsettled frontier zones between rival Celtic tribes.

The hillforts lasted until the Roman occupation when many were destroyed and their inhabitants forcibly resettled in new towns on lower ground. This was the fate of one of the largest and possibly best-known of all these forts, Maiden Castle in Dorset, which was superseded by a new Roman town now called Dorchester. Cheshire's Maiden Castle is on a far more modest scale and less well-preserved than its better-known Dorset namesake but it is still impressive and well worth a visit, both for itself and for the magnificent view.

THE WALK

❶ Start by taking the broad path that leads off from the car park along the inside edge of woodland. Go through a gate, keep ahead steadily uphill and at a junction of paths at the top, continue downhill to reach another gate. Go through, keep ahead to join a track, bear right on joining another track and the track becomes a tarmac lane which continues to a T-junction.

Turn right and follow the winding lane, ignoring all side turns, through the hamlet of Brown Knowl. At a fork about 100 yards beyond a public footpath sign on the right, take the right-hand lane to reach the A534 at a crossroads by the Copper Mine pub at Fuller's Moor.

❷ Turn right along the main road and at a public footpath sign, turn right over a stile and walk across a field to a stile on the far side. Climb it and keep along

The earthworks of Maiden Castle

the right edge of the next two fields. On entering the third field, bear left across it, later continuing along its right edge, and turn right over a stile in the corner. Walk along an enclosed path, turn left over the next stile and keep along the right edge of two fields, finally turning right to a lane. Turn left. Turn right at a T-junction and at a crossroads by Bickerton church, turn right again along Goldford Lane.

❸   At a public footpath sign to Larkton Hill and Whitchurch, turn right onto a tarmac drive, here joining the well-waymarked Sandstone Trail. Go through a kissing gate, head uphill through woodland, go through another kissing gate and keep ahead, climbing steeply at times and passing a succession of superb viewpoints. At a Sandstone Trail fingerpost, turn right, in the Larkton Hill direction, along a sunken track, keep ahead at a crossways, climb steps and continue up to the prehistoric fort of Maiden Castle.

The Iron Age fort of Maiden Castle was built around 600 BC and enclosed an area of around 1.3 acres. On its western side it relied on the natural defence of the cliff edge and on the south and east it was protected by ditches and double ramparts of earth, later strengthened by timber and drystone walling. Some of these ramparts can still be seen. The site was probably occupied until the Roman invasion of Britain in the 1st century AD.

The path heads across the fort along the cliff edge and at a waymark by a Maiden Castle information board, turn right and head downhill. At a fork take the right-hand path to continue more steeply downhill – there are deep steps cut into the rock in places – and at a fingerpost, turn left, in the Hampton and Whitchurch direction, and head down through the trees to a gate. Go through, continue down and at a Sandstone Trail notice board, keep ahead to a T-junction and the car park is just to the right.

REFRESHMENTS

One pub is passed on the route, the Copper Mine at Fuller's Moor. Meals are served from 12 noon – 2 pm and from 6 pm – 9.30 pm and these include a wide variety of lunches, dinners and bar snacks. The pub has an attractive conservatory and a large garden from which there are fine views of the surrounding wooded hills. Tel: 01829 782293

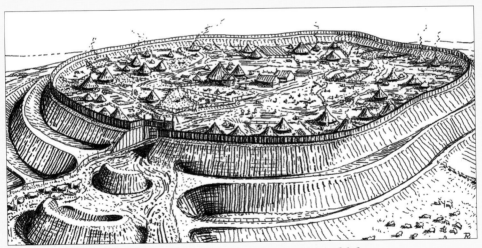

An imaginary Iron Age hillfort showing the complex arrangement of defences
(courtesy of Trevor Yorke)

WALK 2
CHESTER AND THE ROMAN CONQUEST OF BRITAIN

Length: 2½ miles

Chester cathedral

HOW TO GET THERE: Chester has a main-line railway station and is easily reached from the M53, M56 and surrounding main roads.

PARKING: Plenty of pay car parks in Chester city centre

MAP: OS Explorer 266 (Wirral & Chester) GR 405664

INTRODUCTION

This is basically a walk around the walls of Chester, following the circuit in an anti-clockwise direction and making a few digressions from the walls in order to have a closer look at various points of interest, especially those with a Roman theme. Although this is a short walk leave plenty of time, Chester is one of Britain's finest and most interesting historic cities and there is much to see and do.

HISTORICAL BACKGROUND

In 55 BC a Roman army led by Julius Caesar crossed the Channel from Gaul and landed on the south-east coast of England. It hardly penetrated inland but the following year Caesar returned and this time crossed the river Thames and reached about as far north as Hertfordshire. Both visits were brief raids rather than serious invasions and it was not until AD 43 that the Romans returned. This was the start of the conquest of Britain, ordered by the Emperor Claudius.

In the intervening 90 years commercial ties between Britain and the Roman Empire had increased and there was evidence that some of the British tribes were aiding the Gauls in their resistance of the Romans. This was one of the likeliest reasons, along with prestige and a desire for further imperial expansion, for the decision to attempt a conquest of this island on the north-western fringes of the empire.

Unlike the Norman Conquest over a millennium later, the progress of the invaders was relatively slow and steady. From Kent the Romans crossed the Medway and reached the banks of the Thames near London. They then advanced northwards and westwards into south-west England, across the Midlands to Wales, and through northern England and on towards Scotland. The Romans were aided by divisions within the various British tribes and the willingness of some of them to cooperate with them. As they progressed, they built towns, forts and villas, linked by an elaborate system of roads.

There were some setbacks. During Boudicca's revolt in East Anglia in AD 61, the recently established towns of London, St Albans and Colchester were burnt and destroyed and their Roman citizens were slaughtered. The further north and west the Romans advanced the stiffer the resistance they encountered. But Boudicca's rebellion was brutally crushed and under the energetic and ruthless leadership of Agricola, Roman governor of Britain, the conquest was pursued more vigorously into the north, Wales and Scotland. In AD 122, the Emperor Hadrian decided that penetration into Scotland would be too difficult and not worth the effort and therefore he established the northern frontier on the wall that he built between the Tyne and Solway. Later the frontier was briefly pushed further north into the central lowlands of Scotland between the Forth and Clyde and another wall – the Antonine Wall – was constructed but this was soon abandoned and the Romans withdrew back to Hadrian's wall.

In order to maintain control of these more difficult northern and western parts of Britain, the conquerors established three great legionary fortresses. These were Eboracum (York), Isca Silurum (Caerleon) and Deva (Chester). The fort of Chester was built around AD 74–78 on a ridge above the river Dee and overlooking the hills of north Wales.

THE WALK

The walk starts at The Cross, on the site of the Principia or headquarters building, the administrative centre of the Roman fort of Deva and the meeting place of the four main streets that entered the fort. Along all four of the streets are the Rows, the distinctive

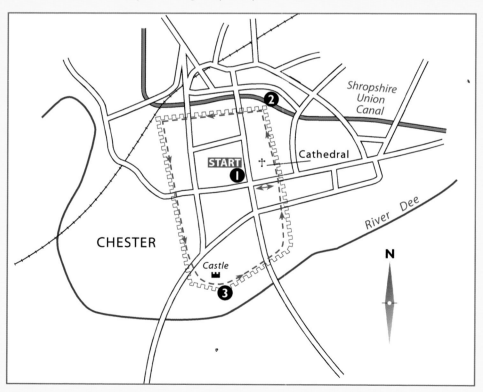

double-storeyed covered walkways that are unique to Chester. Why they are only found here is something of a mystery but as they correspond with the area enclosed within the original Roman defences, one theory is that the medieval builders constructed them on top of the ruins of the Roman buildings instead of levelling them to their foundations.

❶ Facing the late-medieval St Peter's church, turn right along Eastgate Street and pass under Eastgate, surmounted by an ornate clock erected in 1897 to commemorate Queen Victoria's Diamond Jubilee. Eastgate stands on the site of both the medieval and Roman gateways into the town from the east. Immediately turn left up steps to get onto the city walls.

This section is on the line of the original Roman wall and although the walls are mainly medieval, stretches of them, particularly on the northern side, still largely stand on the Roman foundations. As you proceed along them, the cathedral is soon seen over to the left. A brief digression via the modern bell tower brings you to the entrance.

Chester cathedral is built on the site of a variety of Roman buildings, including barrack blocks. The first church was built in the 10th century and this was refounded by the Normans in 1092 as a Benedictine abbey. After the dissolution of the monasteries by Henry VIII it was made the cathedral of a new diocese of Chester in 1541. The cathedral mostly dates from the 14th and 15th centuries and was heavily restored in the Victorian era. The interior is noted for the intricate carvings of the 14th-century choir stalls.

The cathedral retains the layout of the medieval abbey and in many ways the former monastic buildings are its most interesting features. Particularly impressive are the chapter house and refectory, both built in the 13th century. The refectory, which retains the pulpit from which a monk read to the assembled brethren during meals, still appropriately serves its original function as a café.

Return to the wall, either via the bell tower or by the dignified Georgian buildings of Abbey Square and Abbey Street, and continue the circuit. At the north-east corner you come to King Charles' Tower.

The tower, originally known as the Phoenix Tower, gets its name because Charles I is alleged to have watched the defeat of his army from here at the battle of Rowton Moor in 1645. Inside, a small exhibition describes the siege of Chester during the Civil War.

❷ At the corner tower the wall turns westwards, crossing first Northgate and later the modern arch over the inner ring road. Here the Roman wall turned south along the line of the ring road. When the Normans planned their wall, they utilised the crumbling Roman defences but extended them to the river and to include the castle. A little further on at Bonewaldesthorne's Tower the wall turns southwards. Originally the Dee flowed at the base of this tower but as the

Part of the large Roman amphitheatre

river silted up in the 14th century, a new water tower was built at the end of a short spur wall in order to maintain the protection of the harbour. After turning to the south, the wall runs at road level before rising to cross Watergate and then continues at road level again beside the Roodee, Chester's racecourse. Look out for an information panel which tells you that a stretch of the wall of the Roman harbour lies at the base of the medieval wall. Steps lead down to enable you to get a look.

The river Dee has changed its course over the centuries. In Roman times the Roodee racecourse was a tidal pool and ships docked here. Between the harbour and the walls of the fort a large vicus or civilian settlement grew up. The harbour was a thriving one; all kinds of exotic products – wine, olive oil and figs – were brought in from the Mediterranean and slate, silver, lead and roofing tiles – much of it from north Wales – were shipped out to other parts of the empire. A few foundations of the Roman quay wall can be seen at the bottom of the steps.

Continue along the wall to the main road, cross over at the traffic lights and the next stretch of wall runs below the castle.

The great medieval fortress of Chester Castle has all but disappeared. Most of it was rebuilt in the early 19th century in the neo-classical style to serve as barracks, law courts and a prison.

   The original castle was founded in 1069 on a ridge above the river Dee overlooking the hills of north Wales. It was the stronghold of the powerful Earls of Chester and throughout the Middle Ages it was regularly strengthened and updated. During the 13th century in the reigns of Henry III and Edward I, it was the main supply base for military operations against the Welsh and played a key role in Edward I's conquest and subjugation of north Wales. The only remaining medieval buildings are fragments of the walls, parts

> **REFRESHMENTS**
>
> There is such a huge number and variety of coffee shops, restaurants, pubs and wine bars in Chester to suit all tastes that it is virtually impossible to recommend any particular one. However, if you would like to relax with a drink and meal in truly atmospheric and authentic historic surroundings, try the café in Chester cathedral. This is housed in the 13th-century refectory of the medieval abbey and still retains the original preaching pulpit. It serves morning coffee, a range of cooked and light lunches and afternoon tea.
> Tel: **01244 313156**

of some of the towers and in particular the impressive Agricola Tower, the gateway into the inner bailey. Within this tower is the medieval chapel of St Mary de Castro.

❸ By the castle the wall turns eastwards and now comes the only break in it as you have to walk along a short stretch of road in front of County Hall. Climb steps to regain the wall and cross Bridgegate. The original gateway guarded the Old Dee Bridge, until 1832 the only crossing into Wales. After continuing above the river, the wall turns northwards, passing above the Roman Garden, to reach Newgate. Here you descend from the wall in order to visit the Roman Garden, the amphitheatre – the finest of Chester's remaining Roman buildings – and take a look at the foundations of a Roman angle tower.

Architectural fragments from the Roman period found at different places in Chester have been assembled in an imaginative and attractive way in the Roman Garden. These include a colonnade and a hypocaust, an example of the Roman central heating system.

   Nearby and just outside the walls is the amphitheatre, the largest stone-built example yet found in Britain. It was first discovered in the 1920s and only excavated in the 1960s. This was Chester's sports stadium in which between 7000 and 8000 spectators could watch gladiatorial contests, mock battles and various military events. Excavation is ongoing but so far only about half has been uncovered as the other half lies under later buildings.

   Returning to Newgate, on its north side at the base of the wall are the foundations of an angle tower at the south-east corner of the Roman wall.

For the final short stretch back to Eastgate the medieval wall rejoins the line of the Roman wall. At Eastgate descend to street level and retrace your steps to The Cross.

WALK 3
SANDBACH CROSSES AND ANGLO-SAXON ENGLAND

Length: 7 miles

Anglo-Saxon crosses at Sandbach

HOW TO GET THERE: Sandbach is just to the west of Junction 17 on the M6.	PARKING: At the Commons car park on the northern edge of the town centre	MAP: OS Explorer 268 (Wilmslow, Macclesfield & Congleton) GR 758609

INTRODUCTION

From the centre of Sandbach you escape quite quickly and easily into open countryside as you walk across the flat expanses of Sandbach Heath. After passing through Hassall Green, there follows a 1¼ mile stretch beside the Trent and Mersey Canal before the final leg back to the start. There are approximately 14 stiles to negotiate.

HISTORICAL BACKGROUND

The centuries following the withdrawal of the Roman legions from Britain, usually known as the Dark Ages, were a period of uncertainty and confusion. For historians the main problem is a lack of precise evidence, both documentary and archaeological, and therefore much of our knowledge has to be based on conjecture and intelligent guesswork. In the absence of real historical figures, we fall back on legends and mythical characters, such as King Arthur, Vortigern and Hengist and Horsa.

During this misty and confused era the Anglo-Saxons penetrated the country from across the English Channel and North Sea, landing on the south and east coasts and moving inland up the river valleys. Eventually there emerged a number of kingdoms created by the invaders and after much in-fighting, three kingdoms came to dominate the former Roman province of Britain: Wessex in the south, Mercia in the midlands and Northumbria in the north. Wales, Cornwall and Strathclyde (Cumbria and south-west Scotland) remained bastions of the ancient Celtic culture and peoples but the latter two areas also eventually succumbed to the invaders. Boundaries constantly fluctuated as a result of wars between the various Anglo-Saxon kingdoms and between the Anglo-Saxons and the Celts but Cheshire was for most of the time in the Mercian kingdom and Chester was one its chief towns and a major port.

From the end of the 6th century the Anglo-Saxons became converted to Christianity. The conversion process came from two sources: Roman Catholic missionaries from Rome and Celtic missionaries from Ireland and Scotland. By the middle of the 7th century most of England had become Christian.

Towards the end of the 8th century a new threat loomed on the horizon. In 793 the first recorded Viking raid took place on the shores of England, on the Northumbrian island of Lindisfarne or Holy Island. This heralded the beginning of the Viking invasions and by the middle of the 9th century the invaders, mainly from Denmark, had destroyed Northumbria and Mercia. Under the dogged leadership of Alfred the Great, Wessex held out but even Alfred could not drive the invaders back. In 878 he was forced to make a treaty with the Danish leader by which approximately half the country, the north and east, was ceded to the Danes. Cheshire mostly fell within the area under English rule and over the following century Alfred's successors gradually reconquered the area under Danish law and England finally became a united country under a single monarchy.

One of the major problems with Anglo-Saxon England, compared with both the earlier Roman era and the later Norman period, is that there are few remains and in particular few surviving buildings. The Anglo-Saxons mostly built in wood and in the main it was only their churches that were constructed of stone and most of these have disappeared because of later rebuilding and enlarging.

In the absence of buildings we have to rely on the art of the Anglo-Saxons to gain some insight into their culture and way of life and here there are some striking remains. Art flourished in the Anglo-Saxon period and many articles of highly decorated pottery, jewellery and metalwork have been found. After the conversion to Christianity, religious sculpture appeared and a number of religious

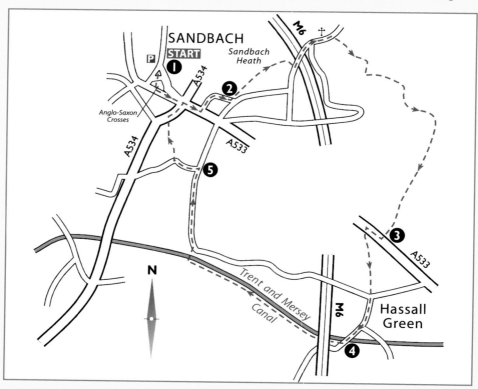

crosses, although in a ruined condition, have survived. The Sandbach Crosses are fine examples of these.

THE WALK

❶ Facing the church and with the library on your left, bear right across the car park and continue along the pedestrianised Penda Way into the cobbled Market Square where the Saxon crosses stand.

There are two crosses – one larger than the other – and they are among the finest examples of their kind in the country, covered with intricate religious carvings. It is believed that they date from the 9th century but according to tradition they were initially erected around 653 on the orders of Peada, son of the Mercian king Penda, to commemorate his conversion to Christianity. His conversion occurred during a visit to Northumbria and the Venerable Bede, the 'father of English history', states that four Northumbrian priests preached at Sandbach and baptised Peada on the spot where the crosses now stand, although this story cannot be verified. After some destruction and mutilation during the 17th century, they were re-erected here in 1816.

The nearby large church dates from around 1633 and was heavily restored in the Victorian era.

Keep ahead to a T-junction and turn left down High Street, passing to the right of the church, to a crossroads. Keep ahead, in the Stoke, Alsager and Newcastle direction, and turn left into Smithfield Lane. Turn right at a T-junction into Hawthorne Drive, following the road around first a left and then a right curve.

❷ At a public footpath sign, turn left along an enclosed path, go down three steps, climb a stile and walk along the right edge of a field. After following the edge around right and left bends, continue across the field towards a church spire. Later keep by a left field edge and in front of a gate turn right to continue along a track to a lane. Turn sharp left, cross a bridge over the M6 and keep ahead towards the church.

The isolated, cruciform church of St John the Evangelist at Sandbach Heath was built in 1861 by George Gilbert Scott, one of the most renowned and prolific of Victorian architects. He designed a host of new churches, was responsible for the restoration of many of England's most outstanding cathedrals and was also the architect of the colossal Midland Hotel at St Pancras station in London.

Where the lane bends left, turn right over a stile and walk across a field to a stile on the far side. Climb it, continue in the same direction across the next field, climb another stile, turn right along an enclosed path through a narrow belt of trees and climb a stile onto a tarmac track.

Turn left, climb a stile, keep ahead and where the tarmac track bends left, climb the stile in front and walk along an enclosed track. Later keep along a left field edge, then curve right to continue along a right field edge, follow the edge to the left – going through a series of gates – keep along a left field edge again and after going through a gate to a footpath post, turn right towards a barn. Go through a gate, keep ahead along an enclosed track, climb a stile and the track later widens and emerges onto a road.

> **REFRESHMENTS**
>
> There are plenty of pubs and cafés at Sandbach and just over half-way round you pass the Romping Donkey pub and a café at Hassall Green. The Romping Donkey, an attractive black and white building, opens for food from 12 noon onwards all day and every day and serves a variety of light and main meals, including a carvery. Tel: 01270 765202

❸ Turn right – take care here as this is a busy road, although there is a verge – and at a public footpath sign, turn left over a stile. Walk along the left field edge, heading down to climb a stile, and turn right along an enclosed track, descending into a dip where you cross a footbridge over a stream. Climb a stile, head quite steeply uphill along the left field edge and continue across the field to climb another stile. Walk along an enclosed track to a road and keep ahead along Smithy Grove into Hassall Green, passing the pub and canalside café.

❹ After crossing the canal bridge, immediately turn right down to the towpath.

The Trent and Mersey Canal was constructed by James Brindley between 1766 and 1777 and linked the river Trent at Shardlow in Derbyshire with the river Mersey at Runcorn in Cheshire, a distance of 93 miles. Among its prominent sponsors was the famous pottery manufacturer Josiah Wedgwood.

Walk along the towpath, passing under the M6, as far as lock 63 and bridge 151. In front of the bridge, turn left through a gap in the wall, turn right and right again to cross the bridge and keep ahead along a road, heading gently uphill towards houses on the edge of Sandbach.

❺ Turn left into Houndings Lane and at a public footpath sign where the lane bends left, turn right along a track. Where the track bends left, keep ahead along an enclosed path to climb a stile and continue along the right edge of a field. After climbing another stile, walk along a path through trees and scrub, bending left towards a stream. Bear right, make your way to the main road and continue along it to a crossroads. Turn left up High Street, here rejoining the outward route, and retrace your steps to the start.

WALK 4
BEESTON CASTLE AND THE DEFENCE OF THE WELSH BORDER

Length: 5 miles

Beeston Castle

HOW TO GET THERE: Bunbury is about ½ mile to the east of the A49 between Tarporley and Whitchurch.

PARKING: Park by the green near the church on the north side of the village

MAP: OS Explorer 257 (Crewe & Nantwich) GR 570582

INTRODUCTION

From the pleasant village of Bunbury the route heads across fields towards the castles of Beeston and Peckforton, occupying similar locations on adjacent wooded hills but around six centuries apart in age. After passing the entrance to Beeston Castle, the return is along lanes and across fields with extensive views all around.

HISTORICAL BACKGROUND

The mountainous terrain of Wales, which had proved to be a problem for the Romans during their conquest of Britain, was also an obstacle for the Anglo-Saxons as they penetrated westwards across the country. Celtic resistance was overcome in Cornwall and Cumbria but not in Wales where the various native princes preserved their independence and from time to time launched raids into England. In the 8th century the great Mercian king Offa constructed a dyke along the length of the border between his territories and Wales to bring some stability to the area but cross-border raids and intermittent warfare continued.

While the Anglo-Saxon kingdoms in England eventually became united, the political situation in Wales was confusing and the Welsh remained divided into a number of separate states under rival and warring leaders. At times Wales became fragmented into weak and small states but occasionally strong leaders emerged who created a greater degree of national unity. One such leader in the 11th century was Gruffudd ap Llywelyn who carried out raids across the border and sacked Hereford in 1055.

The situation changed after the Norman Conquest. After establishing control in England, ambitious Norman barons penetrated into Wales, especially along the coastal lowlands and the river valleys of the south but the mountain interior of Snowdonia proved more difficult. The territories that these barons carved out for themselves along the Welsh border or marches formed a kind of buffer zone between England and Wales and were run as almost independent kingdoms. The Marcher Lords, as they were called, were among the most powerful, ruthless and

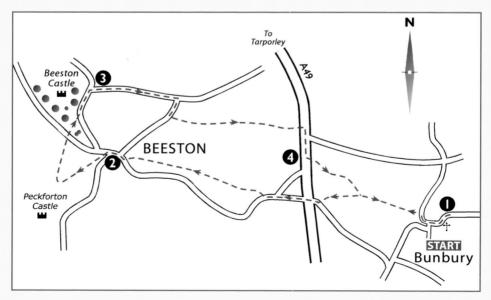

undisciplined of the medieval barons and at times they fought with each other as well as against the Welsh. They were also a major threat to the Crown, sometimes making alliances with the princes of Wales against the English king.

In order to control their newly acquired territories, they built a series of castles stretching from the Dee to the Severn. As Cheshire was in the front line against raids from across the Welsh border, it possessed several of these fortresses. The most important of them was Chester Castle, stronghold of Ranulf, Earl of Chester. In 1225 soon after his return from the Crusades, Ranulf built Beeston Castle as a secondary fortress.

In the early 13th century Wales enjoyed a greater degree of national unity than at any previous time under the rule of the powerful Llywelyn the Great, Prince of Gwynedd (1195–1240). This presented a threat to England and a treaty between Llywelyn and Ranulf in 1218 brought only temporary peace to the border. Warfare resumed and continued on and off over the next half century. Throughout this period Henry III, who had taken control of the Earldom of Chester in 1238 when the male line died out, used Beeston Castle as a base for assembling both troops and supplies for his incursions into Wales. In 1254 he gave it and his other lands in Cheshire to his son, the future Edward I, and since then all heirs to the throne have been granted the title Earl of Chester.

After Henry's death in 1272, Edward I set out to deal with the Welsh menace once and for all. From Chester he launched an attack on north Wales in 1277 and during the ensuing war Llywelyn ap Gruffudd, grandson of Llywelyn the Great and the last native Prince of Wales, was killed in battle in 1282 and his brother David was later captured and executed at Shrewsbury. Welsh independence was extinguished and Wales was fully incorporated into the English administrative system. In order to consolidate his control over the country, Edward built – at enormous expense – the circuit of great castles and walled towns around Snowdonia at Flint, Rhuddlan, Conwy, Beaumaris, Caernarfon and Harlech.

In time these new castles rendered those of the Marches almost obsolete, especially as conditions along the border became more settled and less warlike. It was not only Welsh independence that ended with the conquests of Edward I but also the power and threat of the Marcher Lords.

THE WALK

The village of Bunbury extends over a large area and has a number of attractive old brick-built and half-timbered cottages. The mainly 14th-century church, situated in the upper part of the village near where the walk begins, is unusually large and impressive for a village church. This is because in the late 14th century it became a collegiate church, housing a college or community of canons. Its dominant feature is the 70 ft tower. Inside there are tombs and monuments to several of the prominent local families.

➊ Walk along the road towards the church and where the road bends left by the

The view over Cheshire from Beeston Castle

Dysart Arms, keep ahead along College Lane. At a public footpath sign, turn left over a stile and walk along the left edge of a field, following the edge as it curves left and heads down to a stile.

Climb the stile, continue across a field and just beyond a footpath sign, bear left down to a stile in the corner. Over the stile turn right along the right field edge, climb another stile at a fence corner and keep ahead along a path through trees, climbing two more stiles. After the second one, bear right along the right field edge and the path curves left to a stile. Climb it, walk along an enclosed path, passing between cottages, and continue along a track to a road.

Turn right to the A49 and take the road opposite, signposted to Beeston, and at a public footpath sign to Beeston and Beeston Brook, turn right over a stile. Walk along the left edge of a field, cross a footbridge in the corner and bear slightly left across the next large field, in the direction of Peckforton Castle, making for a stile in a hedge.

Beeston and Peckforton look like twin medieval fortresses crowning neighbouring ridges but Peckforton Castle only dates from the mid-19th century. It was built in the style of a 12th-century castle for John Tollemarche, wealthy landowner and local MP, by the renowned Victorian architect Anthony Salvin. At the time the Gothic Revival was at its height, there was a great interest in anything to do with the Middle Ages and it became fashionable for great country houses to be designed as medieval castles. Some landowners even built mock ruins as a kind of garden ornament to give a suitably romantic appearance to their parklands.

After climbing the stile, continue across the next three fields, finally climbing a stile onto a lane. Turn right. Keep ahead – ignoring side turns – into the hamlet of Beeston.

② Just after the lane curves left, turn right, at a public footpath sign, along a tarmac drive. Continue along an enclosed path through woodland and on emerging from the trees, keep ahead along a path to a T-junction and fingerpost. Turn right here to join the Sandstone Trail. Cross a footbridge, go through a kissing gate, walk along a wide sandy path and go through another kissing gate onto a lane.

Turn left and at a public footpath sign to Delamere and Frodsham, bear right beside a barrier and head uphill through woodland. Bear right alongside a wall on the left to a lane and bear left to the entrance to Beeston Castle.

Standing on top of an abrupt crag over 500 ft above the Cheshire plain, Beeston Castle looks a most imposing and seemingly impregnable fortress but its history reveals that this was not the case and it saw little action. It was built in the early 13th century by Ranulf, Earl of Chester to protect the Welsh border. From its great height, the views extend from the Pennines in the east across to the hills of Wales in the west. The rock itself was a great natural defence and this was augmented by strong walls, towers and two gatehouses, an inner one at the top and an outer one at the bottom of the rock.

In 1238 the Earldom of Chester passed to the Crown and Henry III later gave it to his son, the future Edward I and conqueror of Wales. The castle was used purely as a garrison and unusually was never provided with permanent domestic buildings. Beeston Castle played a part in Edward I's successful campaigns against the Welsh but after the incorporation of Wales into the English administrative system, it became somewhat redundant although it seems to have been kept in good repair until the Tudor period.

Like many English castles, it was patched up and pressed into service during the Civil War when it was seized from its Parliamentary defenders by just a small band of Royalists in 1643. Parliamentary forces retook it after a year-long siege in November 1645, though this was more through starvation than military action. After this its defences were mostly demolished but in recognition of its romantic appearance, the destroyed outer gatehouse was rebuilt in 1846 as a visitor entrance to the ruins. Tel: 01829 260464.

❸ Take the first lane on the right and turn right again at a road. Just before a right bend, turn left over a stile, at a public footpath sign to Bunbury and the A49. Walk along the right edge of a field beside a brook, climb a stile and bear left across the next field to a stile in the far left corner. Climb it, continue along the right edge of the next two fields, climb a stile onto the A49 again and turn right.

❹ At a public footpath sign, turn left over a stile and bear left across a field to climb another stile in the corner. Walk along the left edge of a field, go through a kissing gate and bear left to keep parallel to the left edge of the next field. Where you see a footbridge over the little river Gowy on the left, bear right and head across the field to a stile in the far corner. Climb it and almost immediately turn left over another stile. Here you pick up the outward route and retrace your steps to the start at Bunbury.

WALK 5

DELAMERE AND THE MEDIEVAL ROYAL FORESTS

Length: 4 miles

Delamere Forest

HOW TO GET THERE: The walk starts at the Linmere Visitor Centre in Delamere Forest Park, signposted from the B5152 at Delamere Station.

PARKING: Pay car park at Linmere Visitor Centre

MAP: OS Explorer 267 (Northwich & Delamere Forest) GR 550705

INTRODUCTION

The walk takes you around some of the most popular, attractive and impressive surviving parts of Delamere Forest. Towards the end it passes along the edge of Blakemere Moss, an area of mere and marsh that illustrates one of the main physical features of the forest.

HISTORICAL BACKGROUND

Although some existed in Saxon times, the medieval royal forests of England were basically the creation of the Norman kings. William the Conqueror and most of his successors loved the thrill of the chase and they established a comprehensive network of royal forests scattered throughout the country.

What exactly was a royal forest? Contrary to popular belief, forests were not just large tracts of woodland but any areas set aside for the king as his private hunting ground. They could include villages, towns, open land, farmland, moorland and marsh. Many of the forests of the north and west, such as Bowland and Rossendale in Lancashire and Exmoor and Dartmoor in south-west England, comprised far more open moorland than woodland. Some of the best-known and most visited forests have become embedded in our history and folklore, in particular the New Forest, scene of the death of William II in 1100, and Sherwood Forest, the abode of Robin Hood, Little John, Maid Marian and the rest of the legendary outlaws.

Although principally remembered for the creation of the New Forest, William the Conqueror and his successors designated huge areas of the country as their personal sporting grounds in which they had the sole rights to hunt the 'beasts of the forest', chiefly deer and wild boar. For them the forests were the medieval equivalent of the golf club, a place where they could relax and unwind. A 12th-century chronicler described their appeal in these words: 'thither they repair to hunt, their cares laid aside the while, in order to refresh themselves by a short respite. There renouncing the arduous but natural turmoil of the court, they breathe the pure air of freedom'.

Throughout the royal forests a draconian set of laws was imposed on the inhabitants that were additional to the laws of the realm. Their purpose was to protect both the animals, known as the venison, and the trees and undergrowth that sustained them, known as the vert. Under these laws it was forbidden to hunt or kill any of the protected beasts, fell trees, lop off branches, erect buildings or make clearings without the permission of the king or one of his chief foresters. Penalties for breaking any of these laws were severe, ranging from loss of life or limb for killing one of the royal deer to fines or imprisonment for lesser offences.

All classes of medieval society hated the forest laws. Barons could not hunt in their own woods or chop down their own trees. The clergy disliked them because the laws made no distinction between them and the rest of society. The peasants hated them most of all; they could not collect branches for firewood, extend their plots or dwellings or even prevent the protected deer from trampling over and destroying their vitally needed crops.

At their height in the 12th and 13th centuries the royal forests covered around one third of England and some counties – Essex, Northamptonshire – consisted almost entirely of royal forest. This was obviously a situation that could not last forever. In the later Middle Ages pressures built up – rising social discontent, expensive wars with Scotland and France, increased demands on timber for shipbuilding and the iron industry, and more land needed for agriculture – which led to kings having to reduce the severity of the forest laws and to sell off sizeable chunks of the land. By the end of the medieval period the forest laws had become

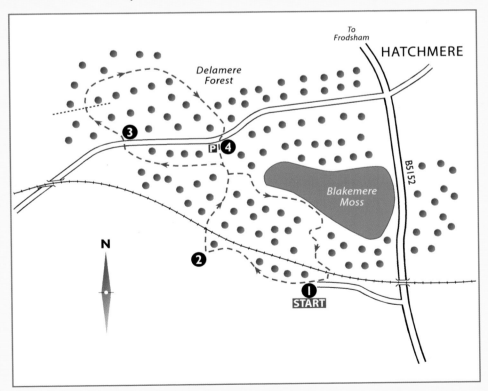

Blakemere Moss in Delamere Forest

largely obsolete and over the following centuries many of the forests ceased to be royal and had most of their trees felled.

Delamere was one of the numerous royal forests in medieval England whose history followed this pattern but unlike some of the others it has survived, albeit on a much smaller scale and with more conifer plantations than ancient oaks and beeches.

THE WALK

In the Middle Ages the adjacent forests of Mara and Mondrum were the hunting grounds of the powerful earls of Chester but when Edward III acquired the earldom in the 14th century, they became royal forests. Their thick woodlands and open heaths covered much of northern and central Cheshire between Nantwich and the river Mersey. Mara was the more northerly of the two, extending to the Wirral and the Mersey; Mondrum stretched southwards towards Nantwich. This forested area was sometimes referred to as the Forest de la Mer (Forest of the Meres) on account of the numerous lakes or meres within its boundaries.

Extensive felling in the 17th and 18th centuries considerably reduced its size and the present Delamere Forest is but a fragment of the great medieval forests, covering around 2400 acres. Nowadays it mainly comprises Forestry Commission conifer plantations but fortunately some impressive broadleaved trees still remain, as this walk will reveal.

1 Turn right out of the car park along a track and at a waymarked post bear right onto a path that keeps by the left edge of trees, following the Baker Way. The path curves right, then bears left and later bends left. After descending into a dip, head uphill to a T-junction.

2 Turn right onto the Sandstone Trail and follow a wide track through the forest. Cross a railway bridge and keep ahead as far as a Delamere Way post where you turn left onto a winding path. Keep along this path to a T-junction and turn right along a track to a road.

3 Cross over, continue along the path opposite and at a crossways, turn right, here leaving the Delamere Way and rejoining the Sandstone Trail. Follow the regular waymarks through the trees and in particular look out for where you are directed to bear right onto a narrower path. Eventually you emerge onto the road again at Barnsbridge car park.

4 Cross over and continue along the track ahead, signposted to Whitchurch and still on the Sandstone Trail. For about 200 yards you rejoin the outward route but at a Delamere Way sign, turn left onto a path which descends to a crossways. Turn right, in the Delamere Way and Linmere direction, and over to the left is the mere and marshy area of Blakemere Moss.

Look out for a fingerpost where you turn left, towards the Visitor Centre, following green-topped posts. At the next crossways, turn right, turn left at a junction and bear left on joining a broad track. After crossing a railway bridge, turn right to return to the start.

WALK 6

TATTON PARK AND THE EVOLUTION OF A LANDED ESTATE

Length: 6½ miles

Tatton Mere

HOW TO GET THERE: Knutsford is just to the east of Junction 19 on the M6.

PARKING: Pay car park, just off King Street, Knutsford

MAP: OS Explorer 268 (Wilmslow, Macclesfield & Congleton) GR 754787

INTRODUCTION

From the centre of Knutsford you soon reach the entrance to Tatton Park. The route then continues along the western side of Tatton Mere to its far end and in order to appreciate how the estate evolved, this is followed by a short circular walk that takes in the Old Hall and its successor, the present Tatton Hall. As a contrast the return to Knutsford is along the more wooded eastern side of the mere. The views across both Tatton Mere and the smaller Melchett Mere and over the open expanses of the 1,000-acre deer park are superb.

HISTORICAL BACKGROUND

The history of Tatton Park is paralleled by that of many other large English country estates but what makes it a particularly illuminating example of how such estates have evolved over the centuries is that the new hall was built on a different site, about ¾ mile to the north-west of the old one. This means that at Tatton there are two halls to visit – widely different in size, standards of comfort and styles of architecture – as the old hall survived instead of being demolished to make way for its successor.

Tatton was originally a small farming community on the edge of Delamere Forest, based around a manor house. Like many villages throughout the country it was badly affected by the Black Death of 1349 which wiped out a large proportion of its inhabitants. The Old Hall dates from around 1500 when the earlier medieval manor house was rebuilt.

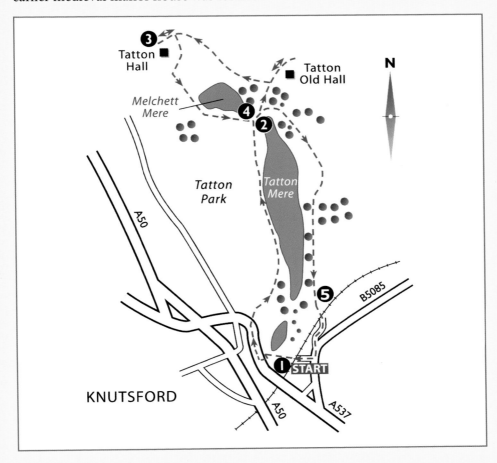

In 1598 the estate was purchased by Sir Thomas Egerton and remained in the possession of the Egerton family for exactly 360 years. Sir Thomas was an able and ambitious man who rose to high office under Elizabeth I and later became Lord Chancellor in the reign of James I. He had other properties and the family had little to do with Tatton until the early 18th century when John Egerton decided to build a new hall. The old hall was subsequently divided into cottages for workers on the estate.

The next major development came in the late 18th century when this new hall was transformed and considerably enlarged by a major building programme carried out for William Egerton. The result was the present imposing grand house, on a par with many such houses both in Cheshire and throughout England. At the same time William Egerton, like many of his fellow landowners, had the park landscaped in the contemporary style with sweeping grassland interspersed with informal areas of woodland, curving driveways and a lake. He commissioned Humphrey Repton, the foremost landscape architect of the day, to carry out the work which – again as elsewhere – included demolishing the village which was next to the old hall and rehousing the inhabitants elsewhere.

Therefore the original small farming settlement based around the old hall became a grand landscaped park dominated by a great house. This continued throughout the 19th century and on into the first half of the 20th century but then the final piece in the jigsaw of Tatton Park is one that is also mirrored in many other great English estates in the second half of the 20th century. With the death of Maurice Egerton in 1958 the family line came to an end and with no male heir, he bequeathed the estate to the National Trust. The present situation is that the National Trust owns the estate but it is administered, maintained and financed by Cheshire County Council.

THE WALK

Before making your way to Tatton Park it is worth spending some time in Knutsford. This interesting and attractive little town has narrow streets, a number of alleyways and a mixture of buildings, including some highly distinctive ones. It is particularly noted for the unique architectural work of the eccentric Richard Harding Watts. His major work is the Gaskell Memorial Tower, part of the King's Coffee House and now the Belle Epoque Restaurant, built in 1907 and passed just after the start of the walk. The tower was built to commemorate the Victorian novelist Elizabeth Gaskell who spent her childhood in Knutsford and based Cranford, *her best-known book, on the town.*

① From the car park walk back up to the road (King Street) and turn right. At a sign, 'Welcome to Tatton Park', bear right along a path between trees and go through the gateway into the park. Turn right along a track which curves left and where it ends keep ahead along a path which heads gently downhill towards Tatton Mere.

Tatton Old Hall

As you continue beside the mere, you enjoy superb views across the water and occasional glimpses of the house. Where the main tarmac drive through the park comes close to the mere, head across the grass to join it and keep along it as far as a gate beside a cattle grid.

❷ After going through the gate, bear right along a grassy path to a tarmac track. Cross it, walk along the tarmac track opposite to Old Hall car park and continue beyond it to the Old Hall.

Tatton Old Hall was originally a timber-framed building later overlain with brick. It dates from around 1500 with 17th- and 19th-century additions. When a new hall was built in the early 18th century, it was abandoned and later converted into three cottages for estate workers. After the last tenant moved out and the estate passed to the National Trust, it was restored as a museum.

The most atmospheric room is the original late-medieval Great Hall with a central hearth and magnificent wooden ceiling. The rest of the hall comprises a series of period rooms that illustrate life in the early 17th century, the Victorian period and finally the 1950s. The hall is approached through the former stable block and there is an old barn on the site. Nearby a few bumps in the ground indicate the site of the former village of Tatton Green. Like many other villages it was seriously depopulated by the Black Death of 1349 and what was left of it was demolished in the 1790s when William Egerton had the park landscaped.

Return to the Old Hall car park, turn right through it and keep ahead along a grassy track to the main drive again. Turn right and follow it as it curves left towards the main car park direction, to the entrance of the present Tatton Hall. In the Stableyard beside the hall there is a restaurant and variety of shops.

Tatton Hall is a grand classical mansion built for William Egerton by Samuel and Lewis Wyatt between 1790 and 1815. It occupies the site of the more modest house built around 1716. The state rooms visited on the tour are full of fine antiques and paintings and there is an extensive collection of furniture made by the renowned Gillow firm of Lancaster. There is also an extensive collection of Egerton family memorabilia and of particular interest is the Tenant's Hall, built by the last occupant of Tatton, Maurice Egerton, a widely travelled man, to house his hunting and other trophies. Now it contains some of his old cars and a collection of curiosities. There is also an impressive library.

Tatton is especially renowned for its 50 acres of ornamental gardens. These include an Italian garden, Japanese garden, fernery, rose garden, walled kitchen garden and Victorian arboretum.

At roughly the same time as the hall was built, the 1,000 acres of parkland, with meres, woodland and herds of deer, was landscaped by Humphrey Repton. He created Tatton Mere but Melchett Mere only appeared in the 1920s as a result of subsidence from nearby salt mining. During the Second World War the park was used for parachute training. Tel: 01565 654822.

③ Retrace your steps a short distance along the drive and by the gates of the hall, bear right onto a worn path that curves gradually right beside the boundary fence of the gardens, heading gently downhill to a gate. After going through it, turn left across the grass towards Melchett Mere and keep by its right edge. At the end of the mere there is a fine view looking back to the façade of the house.

Follow the curve of the mere round to the left and make your way across to the main drive – taking care to avoid the boggy areas – to reach it by the gate and cattle grid passed earlier.

④ Briefly rejoin your outward route by going through the gate and bearing right along a grassy track to a tarmac drive. Turn right along it and at a fork take the right-hand track through trees which continues by the left edge of the park and later curves right into woodland again. Keep on the main track which descends to a kissing gate. After going through, continue in more delightful woodland and go through another kissing gate – here leaving the park.

5 Keep ahead over a railway bridge and on to a road. Walk along the road between houses on the edge of Knutsford to a T-junction. Turn right along Teal Avenue to a main road, turn right and right again into Middle Walk. Head downhill, go under a railway bridge and continue gently downhill along a tarmac path which passes along the end of Moor Pool to a road. The car park is just ahead.

REFRESHMENTS

The centre of Knutsford is packed with restaurants, pubs, wine bars and coffee shops and there is a restaurant in the Stableyard next to Tatton Hall. The Cross Keys Inn, situated close to the starting point, is a pleasantly old-fashioned pub with plenty of character. It serves a variety of full and light lunches – including jacket potatoes, paninis and sandwiches – in relaxing and informal surroundings. Tel: 01565 750404

The Japanese garden in Tatton Park

WALK 7
LITTLE MORETON HALL AND THE RISE OF THE TUDOR GENTRY

Length: 8½ miles

Little Moreton Hall

HOW TO GET THERE: Astbury Mere Country Park is on the western edge of Congleton and is signposted from the A34.

PARKING: Free parking at Astbury Mere Country Park

MAP: OS Explorer 268 (Wilmslow, Macclesfield & Congleton) GR 848626

INTRODUCTION

From Astbury Mere Country Park the route takes you into the village of Astbury and on across fields to the towpath of the Macclesfield Canal. A 1¼ mile stretch by the canal is followed by field paths and tracks which bring you to picturesque Little Moreton Hall. On the return leg to Astbury – across fields and along quiet lanes – there are fine views across to Mow Cop on the horizon and the spire of Astbury church in the middle distance.

HISTORICAL BACKGROUND

The most powerful and wealthy group of people in medieval society were the great landowners, the barons. But in the later Middle Ages and especially during the Tudor period – primarily from around the mid 14th century to the end of the 16th century – the barons found their power increasingly being challenged by the rise of a new class, the gentry or squirearchy.

Who exactly were the gentry? They were basically a rural middle class, lower in status – though not always in wealth – than the titled nobility but higher than the tenant farmers, peasants and landless labourers. They lived in comfortable but relatively modest manor houses, like Little Moreton Hall, rather than in great castles and houses. Their ranks were always being enlarged as ambitious and enterprising small landowners, plus professional men from the towns – merchants and lawyers – were constantly aiming to better themselves and become established in the countryside.

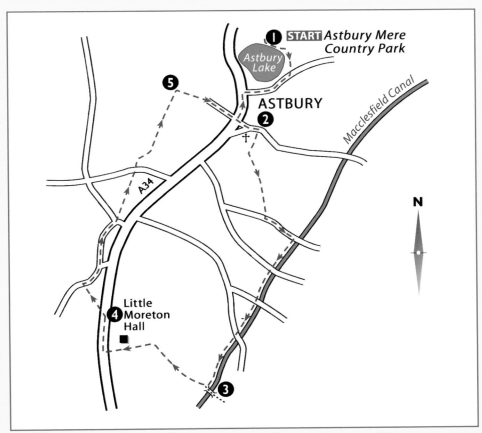

The rise of the gentry started long before the advent of the Tudors. The drastic fall in the population caused by the Black Death (1348–50) led to a surplus of land and some of the smaller landowners – like the Moretons of Little Moreton Hall – seized the opportunity to buy up land cheaply. By the Tudor period they had become relatively large landowners in Cheshire. The Moretons were also clever enough to always be on the right side in order to survive the numerous political upheavals and dynastic changes of the 15th century.

But there were a number of factors in the Tudor era – the 16th century – that particularly favoured the rise of the gentry. Many of the great baronial families of the past had been severely weakened by the Wars of the Roses. After the civil wars their power was curtailed by the emergence of powerful Tudor monarchs who tended to rely more and more on the gentry to fill the important posts in local government, such as sheriffs and justices of the peace. Economic conditions at the time added to their wealth. There was a general rise in rents and prices throughout the 16th century. Many of the gentry converted much of their land to sheep farming and profited from the expansion of the woollen industry. Therefore when large amounts of land came onto the market after the dissolution of the monasteries, many of these enterprising and efficient middle-ranking landowners were in a position to take full advantage of this.

Above all it was Henry VIII's closure of the monasteries and seizure of their estates in the 1530s that accelerated the rise of the gentry. Initially the land went to the Crown but it was subsequently sold off. This heralded the greatest change in land ownership since the Norman Conquest. Much of the land was snapped up by the new landowners and rapidly turned into profitable farming enterprises. The sites of the former monastic buildings were also ideal for erecting new and finer houses as a sign of increased status.

By the end of the 16th century it has been estimated that the gentry owned around 40–50 per cent of the land in England. They were also becoming more numerous and powerful in the House of Commons, a development that was to create a lot of headaches during the 17th century for Elizabeth I's Stuart successors. The great historian G.M. Trevelyan summed it up in these words: 'Elizabeth's reign was a great age for the gentry. Their numbers, wealth and importance had been increased by the decay of the old nobility that had stood between them and the Crown; by the distribution of the monastic estates; and by the vitality of commerce and land improvement in the new era.'

THE WALK

❶ Begin by heading down to the mere along a well-surfaced path which bends left to continue alongside it. At a fork by the corner of the mere, take the left-hand upper path, ascend steps and turn right up more steps to a T-junction. Turn right, bend left, keeping above the mere, and the path emerges onto a lane called Fol Hollow. Turn right to the A34, turn left into Astbury and turn left again alongside the triangular village green, keeping to the left of the church.

In a county noted for its imposing medieval churches, Astbury is one of the most impressive and certainly one of the most unusual. Instead of being in line with the nave and chancel, the tower and spire rise above the north-west corner and appear to be almost detached from the main body of the church. It dates mainly from the 13th to 15th centuries and the spire is a prominent landmark for miles around. The church is wide and spacious with some fine wood carvings.

❷   At a public footpath sign, climb a stile and turn right along the right edge of a field. Climb a stile, walk across the next field and climb another stile in the right-hand corner. Turn left along the left field edge, climb a stile, head straight across the next field and climb a stile in the far right-hand corner.

The dramatic ruin that can be seen on the skyline ahead at this point is Mow Cop Castle. Despite its name it is not a castle but an 18th-century folly, built by a local landowner as a summer house and to improve his view. It is in sight for much of the walk.

Walk along the left field edge, climb a stile, continue in the same direction across the next field and cross a plank footbridge in the corner. Keep ahead, climb a stile onto a lane and turn left. In front of an aqueduct turn right up steps, climb a stile and turn right along the towpath of the Macclesfield Canal. Keep along it for about 1¼ miles as far as bridge 86.

The Macclesfield Canal, constructed between 1826 and 1831, runs for 26 miles across Cheshire from its junction with the Peak Forest Canal at Marple to where it joins the Trent and Mersey Canal at Kidsgrove. It was built to serve the industries around Bollington, Macclesfield and Congleton and to provide a link between Manchester and the Midlands.

❸   After passing under bridge 86, turn right through a kissing gate, keep ahead to go through another one and turn left along a track. Curve left to enter a field, keep along its right edge, climb a stile and continue along the right edge of the next field. After climbing a stile in the corner, bear left across a field to another stile. Climb it, cross a track, climb the stile opposite and continue along the right field edge. Climb another stile and keep ahead along a tarmac track to Little Moreton Hall.

Whether you have been here before or not, it is more than likely that you have already seen Little Moreton Hall as its picture adorns thousands of greetings cards and calendars.

Approaching Astbury on the return leg

With its black and white timber-framing, higgledy-piggledy appearance and moat, it is everyone's idealised picture of what an old English manor house should look like. It belonged to the Moreton family, local landowners who first became rich by buying up land cheaply after the Black Death and becoming loyal tax collectors for the king.

The house was built in stages. The earliest part is the great hall, constructed around the middle of the 15th century. In the second half of the 16th century came first the east wing and finally the south wing. The latter includes the gatehouse and above it was built a third storey that comprised a long gallery, 68 ft in length, built there because there was no space to have it anywhere else. It is this gallery that is responsible for much of the irregular appearance of the hall as its weight has caused the south front to sag.

As staunch Royalist supporters, the fortunes of the Moretons declined after Parliament's victory in the Civil War and the house declined with them, falling into a dilapidated condition. Its picturesque qualities were recognised in the Victorian era and a programme of restoration was begun. Since 1938 the hall has been owned and maintained by the National Trust. Tel: 01260 272018.

Continue along the track to the A34, cross over and turn right along the footpath.

❹   After about ¼ mile – and about 200 yards beyond the entrance to Cuttleford Farm – turn left over a stile, at a public footpath sign, and walk along the left edge of a field. At a hedge corner, continue across the field and then keep along the right edge of the next field to emerge onto a road.

Turn right and where the road curves right to the main road, bear slightly left to continue along a narrow lane (Brook Lane). At a T-junction, turn left and where the road bears slightly left, bear right, at a public bridleway sign, along a broad tarmac track. Where the tarmac ends, keep ahead along a straight tree-lined track to a road.

> **REFRESHMENTS**
>
> The Egerton Arms at Astbury overlooks the church and triangular village green and is situated about 1 mile from the start of the walk. The inn dates from the 15th century and does a full range of cooked meals in the restaurant and a wide selection of bar meals and snacks. Tel: 01260 273946

Cross over, take the tarmac track ahead and at a crossways and fingerpost, turn right along an enclosed track. Keep along this winding track, enjoying fine views of Astbury church and the hills on the horizon. Ignore all side turns and later continue along the right edge of a field to a stile. Climb it – and another one immediately ahead – walk across the next field and climb a stile onto a tarmac track.

⑤ Turn right, climb a stile and the track becomes a lane which emerges onto the A34 almost opposite Astbury church. Turn left, here rejoining the outward route, and retrace your steps to the start.

WALK 8

BATTLE OF NANTWICH AND THE ENGLISH CIVIL WAR

Length: 5 miles

The Shropshire Union Canal cuts across the heart of the battle site at Nantwich

HOW TO GET THERE:
Nantwich is situated on the A534 just to the south-west of Crewe.

PARKING: Plenty of pay car parks in Nantwich

MAP: OS Explorer 257 (Crewe & Nantwich) GR 652524

INTRODUCTION

The first part of the walk between Nantwich and Acton takes you along the towpath of the Shropshire Union Canal, from where there are wide and unimpeded views across the fields that were the site of the battle. From Acton the route continues across fields with a final stretch beside the river Weaver.

HISTORICAL BACKGROUND

The English Civil War between king and Parliament officially began on 22 August 1642 when Charles I raised his banner outside the walls of Nottingham Castle but the country had been drifting into war for some time. Although its origins and causes are complex and varied, it was basically a struggle for power. The king believed he ruled by divine right, by the will of God, and this enabled him to do as he pleased. Parliament on the other hand believed that it represented the will of the English people and was entitled to a share in the government.

Quarrels in the early part of his reign led Charles to dissolve Parliament in 1629 and rule the country on his own for eleven years. Constitutionally he was within his rights but Parliamentarians were naturally furious and called this period 'The Eleven Years' Tyranny'. In order to raise money and escape dependence on Parliamentary taxation, Charles resorted to some dubious methods, including forced loans and the imposition of Ship Money, a tax on towns to raise funds for the navy at time of war. He also angered Parliament, many of whose members were Puritans, by attempting to enforce a High Church form of Anglicanism.

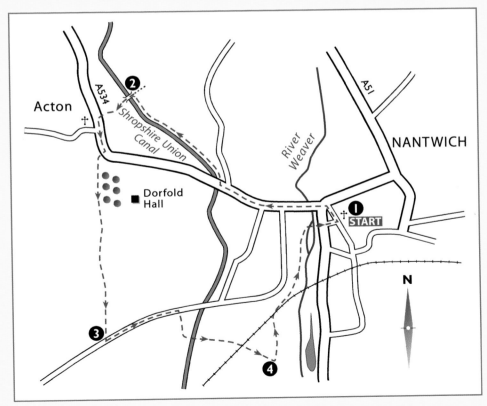

His attempt to force bishops and the Church of England Prayer Book on his predominantly Presbyterian subjects in Scotland led to war with the Scots and a severe shortage of money. Unable even to pay his troops, Charles was reluctantly forced to recall Parliament in 1640. Many of its members were in an angry and sullen mood and determined to ensure that no king could ever again ignore them for such a long time. Relations between the two sides deteriorated rapidly and for many Parliamentarians the last straw was when Charles marched into the House of Commons in January 1642 to arrest five members whom he regarded as the chief troublemakers. He failed – they had been tipped off – but from then on both sides began preparing for war.

The country was divided; in general the south and east supported Parliament and the north and west – including Cheshire and Wales – was for the king. Initially the king had the better-trained and more experienced army but Parliament controlled the capital, most of the ports and the more heavily populated areas. An alliance with the Scots in 1644 and the military genius of Oliver Cromwell tipped the balance decisively in Parliament's favour and a succession of Parliamentary victories between 1644 and 1646 led to the eventual surrender of the Royalists and the imprisonment of the king. In 1649 Charles was executed for high treason and the monarchy was abolished.

THE WALK

❶ The walk starts in the town centre by the war memorial and in front of the impressive medieval church.

Nantwich's cruciform church, often justifiably described as the 'cathedral of south Cheshire', is a reflection of the wealth of the town in the Middle Ages, a wealth based on the salt industry. It dates mainly from the 14th century and was comprehensively restored in the Victorian era. Externally the most striking feature is the octagonal central tower but inside its chief glory is the chancel, noted for its 14th-century vaulting and magnificent choir stalls, a riot of complex and intricate woodcarving of a quality usually only seen in some of the cathedrals. In the tumultuous events of 1644 it served as a temporary prison for Royalist prisoners captured at the battle of Nantwich.

With your back to the church, turn right along the pedestrianised High Street. Bear left on reaching a road, keep ahead to cross the bridge over the river Weaver and continue along Welsh Row to the canal aqueduct. Climb steps up to the towpath and turn right.

The Shropshire Union Canal was one of the last to be built, completed in 1835 just at the time when competition from the railways was starting. Thomas Telford was the engineer and it ran from the edge of Wolverhampton, where it linked up with the Staffordshire and Worcestershire Canal and the Birmingham canal system, to the river

Nantwich town centre

Mersey at Ellesmere Port. The canal is the major feature of the surrounding landscape that did not exist at the time of the battle. The battle was fought on the flat fields either side of the canal, predominantly on those to the east stretching towards the A51.

During the Civil War Cheshire was predominantly in Royalist hands and by the end of 1643 the Royalist commander Lord Byron controlled most of the county except for Nantwich, which had a Parliamentary garrison commanded by Sir George Booth. Byron was determined to rectify that situation, advanced on the town with around 5000 troops and began a siege in December 1643. Fairfax, the leading Parliamentary commander, set off to relieve Nantwich.

Byron divided his army. Most of his troops were on the west bank of the river Weaver at Acton but some were sent on to the east side, crossing the river by a temporary bridge on the site of the present Beam Bridge where the A51 crosses the Weaver. Bad weather on the night of the 24 January 1644 caused the river to burst its banks and the bridge was swept away, destroying the main avenue of communication between the divided Royalist forces.

On the following day Byron stationed his infantry in front of Acton church and personally took command of the cavalry. Meanwhile Fairfax was marching to the relief of the town along the line of the A51. The two armies fought in the fields to the west of Nantwich, between Acton and the present A51. Both sides were hampered by poor visibility and in the confused and fierce hand-to-hand fighting, it was literally every man for himself. The waterlogged ground and the presence of numerous hedgerows across the battle site rendered the superior Royalist cavalry largely ineffective and Fairfax was also helped by the fact that many of the Irish troops in Byron's army deserted to him.

The Royalists were soundly defeated. Most of the cavalry retreated to Chester but around 1500 infantry troops were driven back towards Acton church where they surrendered. It was a severe blow to the Royalist cause as the battle ended their domination of Cheshire.

❷   After passing under bridge 93 (Acton Bridge) turn right up steps and the path bends right to cross the bridge. Go through a kissing gate, walk across a field, go through another gate and continue along an enclosed tarmac path to a road. Bear right to a T-junction and turn left along the main road through the village of Acton, passing the church and the Star Inn.

Acton church dates mainly from the 13th and 14th centuries but the imposing tower had to be partially rebuilt after the top part of its predecessor was blown down during a gale in 1757. In 1644 the church was used as a base by the Royalist army at the start of the battle and it was here that many of the defeated and exhausted Royalist infantry surrendered to the Parliamentary victors at the end of the battle.

Just beyond the pub – and before the road bends left – bear slightly right to walk along a track through trees and continue along the track, passing beside several gates, to reach a lane. Keep ahead to a road.

3 Turn left and after almost ½ mile – and about 200 yards beyond a public footpath sign to the right – turn right along a narrow lane which bends left to cross a bridge over the canal. Here the lane bends right but the route continues ahead through a gate and along the right edge of a field. Go through a gate, walk along an enclosed path, carefully cross a railway line, go through another gate and keep along a right field edge. Go through two gates in quick succession and continue along the left field edge.

> **REFRESHMENTS**
>
> There is a good selection of pubs, cafés and wine bars in Nantwich. An interesting and atmospheric place in which to relax is the Nantwich Bookshop Coffee Lounge on the first floor above the bookshop, housed in two black and white Tudor buildings built – like so many in the town – in the 1580s following a great fire. It is open Monday–Saturday from 9 am to 4.30 pm and serves morning coffees, afternoon teas, and a variety of sandwiches, baguettes, salads and jacket potatoes.
> Tel: 01270 611665

4 After about 100 yards look out for a stile and turn left over it. Walk across a field to a waymarked stile, climb it and veer slightly left towards the left field edge where you climb two stiles in quick succession. Cross a grassy strip to climb another stile, bear right across the next field, climb a stile, cross a track and head up a slight embankment to the railway line again. Re-cross the line, immediately turn right over a stile and walk along the right field edge parallel to the embankment.

Climb a stile in the corner, cross a plank footbridge and keep ahead through trees to join a grassy track which curves left to continue beside the river Weaver. Keep ahead on joining a tarmac path, following signs to 'Town Centre', and at a T-junction turn right to cross a bridge over an arm of the river. The path bends first left and then right and crosses another arm of the river to emerge onto a road. Cross over, keep ahead along Mill Street to emerge onto High Street and the starting point is just to the left.

WALK 9

PARKGATE AND THE RISE AND FALL OF THE DEE ESTUARY PORTS

Length: 4½ miles

Parkgate

HOW TO GET THERE: Parkgate is signposted from the A540 between Heswall and Neston; the Old Baths car park is at the north end of the village.

PARKING: Old Baths car park at Parkgate

MAP: OS Explorer 266 (Wirral & Chester) GR 274790

INTRODUCTION

The first part of the route is through the former port of Parkgate and along the edge of the extensive marshes of the Dee estuary, from where there are fine and extensive views across the river to the hills of north Wales. This is followed by a walk along the Wirral Way and a short stretch along a parallel and slightly higher track, from which the views over the estuary are even more spectacular.

HISTORICAL BACKGROUND

The rise and fall of the ports on the Dee estuary is primarily bound up with the silting up of the river. As the Dee continued to silt up, the ports moved progressively further and further downstream until finally commercial activity moved away from the Dee altogether to the Mersey and the port of Liverpool.

Roman Chester was the first of the Dee estuary ports. Although primarily a vital military stronghold, the fort of Deva was also one of the most important ports in Roman Britain. After the departure of the Romans, Chester's importance as a port increased and in the Middle Ages it became the chief port of north-west England. It traded extensively across the Irish Sea with Dublin and with both France and Spain. It was also used as a launching pad and supply point for invasions by sea of both Wales and Ireland.

The silting up of the Dee was a long and gradual process but by the end of the Middle Ages, Chester's commercial greatness had declined and ports started to

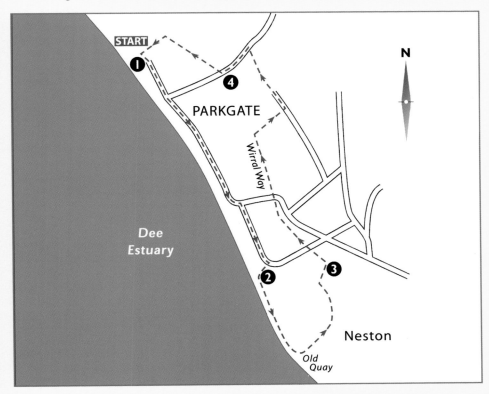

develop further down the estuary. The village of Burton was the first successor. It had developed into a small but prosperous port by the 14th century but declined for the same reason as Chester. Then the main port shifted further down to Neston where a new quay was established in the 1540s and the town became a thriving and prosperous port. It had coaching links with London and was a major point of departure for Ireland, Spain and France. In the 18th century a colliery was sunk near Neston and coal was shipped from here across the estuary to north Wales and over to Ireland.

The silting up of the river was accelerated by the building of the New Cut in the 1730s when the Dee was straightened and canalised. This had the effect of diverting the water from the northern (Wirral) side of the estuary to the southern (Welsh) side. Not only did it bring about the decline of Neston but it ensured that its successor, Parkgate, had a relatively short life. During the 18th century Parkgate enjoyed a heyday as a commercial and passenger port but it too suffered the same fate as its predecessors. In an attempt to prolong its life, it became a holiday resort but this also failed as the waters of the estuary retreated and the thick marsh expanded further.

The silting up of the river was not the only problem for the ports on the Dee. It was always a shallow and rather unpredictable river and was unsuited to take the larger vessels. In particular the advent of the steamships in the 19th century was a major blow. The Mersey was deeper and, as the Industrial Revolution gathered pace, had the advantages of being closer to the coalfields of south Lancashire and better placed to handle both the growing textile trade and passenger traffic.

By the middle of the 19th century the Dee was finished commercially. As one writer put it: 'Nature and the Industrial Revolution between them assisted and established the supremacy of the Mersey, virtually reducing the Dee as a line of communication to a nonentity'. In the long run the main beneficiaries of the decline of commercial traffic and ports on the Dee were the ports on the Mersey. But for the vagaries of the river Dee, Chester, Neston or Parkgate might have developed into another Liverpool.

THE WALK

❶ Facing the estuary, turn left along the road to the Boat House and continue into Parkgate.

With its attractive promenade, collection of whitewashed cottages and half-timbered buildings, Parkgate has a pleasantly old-fashioned air. It was established as a port in the early 18th century when the silting up of the River Dee caused the earlier ports to decline and necessitated the development of new ports further downstream. Previously it had been little more than an appendage of Neston, its immediate predecessor.

Parkgate was at its height in the 18th century when it was a busy port. Frequent

The remains of the old quay at Neston

ferries sailed across the Dee to Flint in north Wales and there was a flourishing passenger trade with Ireland. It is reputed that Handel added the final touches to the Messiah *while staying here in the 1740s on his way to Dublin for the first performance of that great work. At that time it possessed a theatre, customs house, assembly rooms, inns, gambling parlours and coffee houses.*

In the 19th century Parkgate suffered the same fate as Chester and the other Dee ports as the silting up of the river continued relentlessly. A sign of its decline was that by the 1830s the packet boat service to Dublin had ceased and moved to Liverpool. It had a brief period as a fishing port and later became a popular seaside resort. The Old Baths, the remains of which were passed at the start of the walk, were built in 1923 for the enjoyment of holidaymakers and at the time were regularly washed by seawater. But within a decade the water had receded further and the baths were finally closed in 1942. Now the promenade overlooks acres of thick marsh and the hills of north Wales.

After passing the main buildings on The Parade, turn left along Station Road and take the first road on the right (Manorial Road). Follow it around right and left bends and where the road ends, keep ahead along a fence-lined track. Continue along Manorial Road South and where it bends left, turn right along an enclosed path back to the estuary.

2 The path bends left and keeps along the edge of the marshes to a stile. Climb it and walk along the right edge of a field, passing a few scanty remains of a former quay.

These blocks of stone are all that remain of the quay at Neston, Parkgate's predecessor as a Dee estuary port. From here Flint Castle in north Wales can be seen on the other side of the estuary.

Cross a plank footbridge over a brook and continue to a stone stile. Do not cross it but turn left onto a stony path – later with a hedge on the right – to a kissing gate. Go through, cross a plank footbridge and keep ahead across a field, curving left along what is now an enclosed path to go through another kissing gate onto a tarmac track. Keep ahead and at a public footpath sign turn right along an enclosed path to a crossways.

3 Turn left onto a track, here joining the Wirral Way, and on emerging into a car park keep ahead to a road on the edge of Parkgate.

For the Wirral Way see walk 11.

Turn right and where the road bends right, turn left, at a Wirral Country Park sign, beside a gate onto a track. After crossing a road bridge, turn sharp right down to the road and bear left along an enclosed track to a lane. Turn left and the lane becomes a rough track which continues to a road. Turn left towards the estuary.

4 After crossing a bridge, turn right down steps and turn left to rejoin the Wirral Way. In front of the next bridge, turn right up steps, turn left over the bridge and walk along an enclosed path back to the car park.

WALK 10
STYAL AND THE TEXTILE INDUSTRY
Length: 4½ miles

Norcliffe Chapel at Styal

HOW TO GET THERE: The entrance to Styal Country Park is off the B5166 to the south of Manchester Airport and to the north of Wilmslow. Follow signs to Quarry Bank Mill and Styal Country Park from M56, A538 and B5166.

PARKING: Pay car park at Styal Country Park

MAP: OS Explorer 268 (Wilmslow, Macclesfield & Congleton) GR 835830

INTRODUCTION

The twin focal points of Styal Country Park are Quarry Bank Mill and the adjacent Styal village, both built by the Greg family, the mill owners. The water power provided by the river Bollin was one of the main motives for building the mill here. Apart from the mill and village, the park mainly comprises the beautiful, steep-sided Styal Woods that slope down to the river. Walking through here is one of the chief delights of the route.

HISTORICAL BACKGROUND

Since the Middle Ages wool had been England's chief industry but in the early 18th century cotton became a rival, growing rapidly and later outstripping wool in production. Not only was it the fastest growing industry in England during the Industrial Revolution, it was also the industry that pioneered both new machinery and new methods of working. Previously most textile workers had worked in their own homes using simple hand-operated machines. The work was distributed to them and later collected when finished. This was known as the domestic system.

The new methods were themselves the necessary consequence of the growth of water-powered machines, such as Arkwright's Water Frame and Crompton's Mule. The workers could no longer work at home but had to come to work in mills or factories. These were essentially sheds that housed the machinery and were mainly situated on the banks of streams where the power of the water could be harnessed to drive the new machines. Thus the factory system was born.

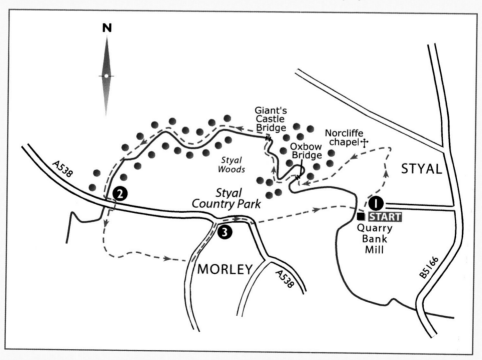

Cotton was the most geographically concentrated industry in Britain. Over 90 per cent of cotton production became located within a 20–30 mile radius of Manchester. One of the major reasons for this was the proximity of the port of Liverpool, through which both the raw cotton from America was imported and the finished products were exported. Other factors included the damp climate (good for preventing the cotton thread from breaking), plenty of fast flowing streams to provide the water power, coal supplies in the locality when steam-powered machines later superseded those powered by water, and a workforce skilled in textile manufacturing from the earlier woollen industry.

Textile mills rapidly sprang up throughout the area. Most of them were in south Lancashire but a number were established in north Cheshire to the south of Manchester. From the start Quarry Bank Mill at Styal was rather different from the norm. It was a new site in a rural and thinly-populated area with only a few cottages in the vicinity. Samuel Greg, the owner, needed to attract workers to his vast new mill and to do this he provided houses for them that were superior to most working-class housing at the time.

Samuel Greg was strict and far from being a soft-hearted, enlightened employer. The working hours at Styal were long, wages were low, discipline was harsh and Greg made full use of cheap child labour. Despite this, his provision of decent housing conditions – at least compared with contemporary Manchester and Liverpool – plus a shop, churches, medical and educational facilities, was in advance of its time and was to be a blueprint for future new industrial communities at New Lanark, Saltaire, Bournville and – fairly close by – Port Sunlight (see walk 14).

Quarry Bank Mill thrived during the heyday of cotton throughout the Victorian era and up to the outbreak of the First World War but, like the rest of the industry, it fell on hard times during the great depression of the 1920s and 30s. In 1939 the Gregs gave the mill, Styal village and the adjacent woods to the National Trust, the mill ceased commercial production twenty years later and the whole site is now a fascinating museum.

THE WALK

In 1784 Samuel Greg, a cotton manufacturer from Manchester, built Quarry Bank Mill on the banks of the swift flowing river Bollin at Styal, a small agricultural settlement near Wilmslow. Over the following years the spinning mill prospered and was extended. It expanded further in the 1830s when Robert Greg, Samuel's son, added weaving sheds and in its heyday it employed over 400 workers.

The mill is a striking building and clearly illustrates that industrial structures do not have to be ugly and badly designed. One of its most attractive features is the bell tower, though this was added for purely ulterior motives to ensure good timekeeping among the workforce.

Samuel Greg's main problem was that the neighbouring village was too small to

Some of Samuel Greg's cottages at Styal

provide the workforce he required for the mill and therefore he had to recruit workers from outside the area, including pauper children. He also had to provide accommodation for both his family and his employees. He built houses for himself and his family and for the mill manager close to the mill and a little further away the Apprentice House, which is passed soon after the start of the walk, was erected in 1790. This housed around 60 pauper apprentices sent here from various workhouses. The child apprentices not only provided the Gregs with a cheap and plentiful labour supply but relieved the local parishes from where they came from a burden on the rates. The garden around the Apprentice House has been made into a Victorian allotment.

Since being given to the National Trust and ceasing commercial production, Quarry Bank Mill has become a museum with a working waterwheel – brought from elsewhere – and there are practical demonstrations of textile machinery and displays on how people lived and worked here during the Industrial Revolution. Tel: 01625 527468.

❶   Exit the car park, passing the pay kiosk, and just before the drive curves right, turn sharp left by the entrance to the Apprentice House – almost doubling back. At a sign to Styal Village, turn right along an enclosed path, go through a gate, keep ahead, go through another gate and turn right along a hedge-lined track into the village.

The few, old, half-timbered cottages that made up the small and scattered hamlet of Styal were obviously incapable of housing the large workforce at the mill and Samuel Greg was forced to provide housing for them. The result was a purpose built factory village with rows of cottages, mostly dating from the early 19th century, that were far in advance of most workers' housing at the time, with individual privies and back gardens. He also founded a school for local and factory children in 1823, set up a village shop, employed a doctor and, as a good Unitarian, also catered for the spiritual needs of his workers and their families. At first the nearest place of worship entailed a walk across the fields to Wilmslow church but in 1822 Greg – like many industrialists he was a Nonconformist – built the Unitarian Oak Chapel (later renamed the Norcliffe Chapel) and in 1837 a wagon house at Farm Fold was converted into a Methodist chapel.

The mill and village together make up an unusually complete and rare example of a self-contained early Industrial Revolution mill community, almost entirely the creation of one man. And because of its relative isolation from the main sources of power and centres of population in Victorian England, it has been largely unspoilt by later developments.

Turn left in front of the Methodist church and where the track bends right, keep ahead along an enclosed path in front of cottages, curving left to a junction of paths by the medieval Styal Cross. Keep ahead towards Norcliffe Chapel and just before the lych gate of the chapel, pass beside a barrier on the left and walk along an enclosed path. Pass beside another barrier, cross a track and keep ahead to enter Styal Woods.

These delightful woods that clothe the steep banks of the river Bollin were planted by Robert Greg in the middle of the 19th century.

At a fork immediately ahead, take the left-hand path which descends quite steeply to the river Bollin. Cross Kingfisher Bridge over a tributary stream, keep by the river on the left, at a fork take the left-hand path and just after following the Bollin around a right bend, turn left over Oxbow Bridge. Turn left along the other bank of the river. At this point the river is briefly on both sides of the path as this is the narrowest point of a horseshoe bend.

Continue up a flight of steps, keep ahead above the valley and the path descends, via more steps, to continue by the Bollin, now on your right. Follow it around left and right curves and, where the river bends left again, re-cross it by Giant's Castle Bridge. Immediately climb a long flight of steps and continue along the right inside edge of the trees. Descend steps again, turn right to cross a bridge over a stream at the bottom and continue with the river now on the left. The path emerges from the trees but soon after passing a bridge on the left, plunges once more into woodland. The path winds through what is arguably the most beautiful part of Styal Woods, climbs above the river, descends again and eventually emerges onto a tarmac track, here leaving the country park. Turn left, crossing the Bollin again, and walk through the car park of the Holiday Inn to the A538.

❷ Cross over, turn right and at a public footpath sign, turn left through a kissing gate. Walk across a field, cross a footbridge and keep ahead. Go through a kissing gate and head up a wooded embankment, curving left to another kissing gate. Go through, continue across a field and on the far side, descend steps to cross a footbridge. Head up to a fingerpost and turn left. Keep by the left edge of a field, climb a stile and keep ahead along an enclosed path which emerges onto a parallel track. Follow the track to a road and turn left through the hamlet of Morley to the A538 again.

❸ Turn right along the main road and where it curves right, turn left to cross it and take the enclosed track ahead, signposted as a restricted byway. Go through a gate, keep ahead, go through another gate beside a farm building and bear slightly left to continue along a delightful path above the valley, between a wire fence on the left and a line of trees on the right.

After going through a gate, the path descends to cross the river Bollin by Quarry Bank Mill. Head up by the side of the mill, turn right to continue in front of it and steps on the left lead back to the car park.

WALK 11
THE WIRRAL WAY AND THE RAILWAY AGE

Length: 5½ miles

Hadlow Road station

HOW TO GET THERE: Hadlow Road station is off the B5151 on the southern edge of the village of Willaston which is between Neston and the M53; follow Wirral Way signs from the village centre.

PARKING: Hadlow Road station

MAP: OS Explorer 266 (Wirral & Chester) GR 331774

INTRODUCTION

The Wirral Way, which follows the line of a former railway, is the focal point of this highly attractive walk. It starts at a former station, frozen in a 1950s time warp, and at the approximate half-way point there is the opportunity to visit an attractive botanic garden. Along the route there is a succession of fine views over surprisingly quiet, open and unspoilt countryside.

HISTORICAL BACKGROUND

Britain's railways originated in the coal mines of the north-east where in the 18th century horse-drawn wooden wagonways were constructed to transport coal trucks from the mines to the nearest rivers. With the development of steam power, pioneers began experimenting with devising a steam engine that could haul the wagons. One such pioneer was George Stephenson and in 1825 his engine *Locomotion No 1* was used on the new Stockton to Darlington Railway. This carried passengers and was the first steam-hauled public railway but it was not entirely steam-operated and still relied at times on horse power.

A company was set up to build a railway between Liverpool and Manchester and in 1829 the directors of the company held trials at Rainhill to decide whether to use stationary steam engines or locomotive engines on their new line. Five engines took part in these Rainhill Trials and the winner was George Stephenson's *Rocket* which reached the unheard of speed of around 30 mph. The opening of

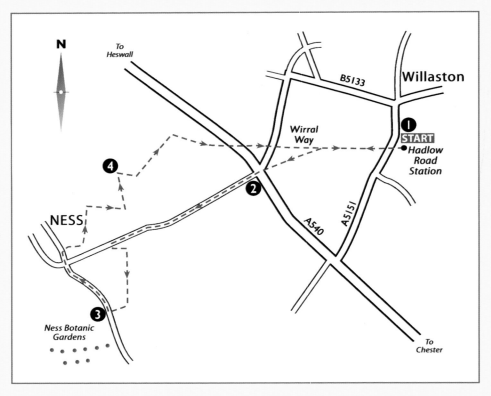

the Liverpool to Manchester Railway in 1830, the world's first passenger railway, is the event generally acknowledged as marking the start of the Railway Age.

The speed and noise of these new iron monsters terrified many superstitious people who were to claim in later years that the railways were responsible for such catastrophes as farm animals being born deformed and cows being unable to produce milk. The opening of the railway itself was marred by the world's first rail fatality when William Huskisson, MP for Liverpool and President of the Board of Trade, was struck by the locomotive and died. Despite these setbacks, doubts and forebodings the railways prospered and over the following twenty years, the peak of the Railway Age, lines were built all over the country linking all the major towns and cities in a remarkably short time. Later branch lines were extended into the rural areas and by the late 19th century even the remotest places – East Anglia, the south-west, Wales, northern England and the Scottish Highlands – were not far from a railway line. In many ways these areas were less cut off in the Victorian era than nowadays, since the wholesale closures of rural lines in the 1960s. The Wirral line, which provided an additional link between Chester and Liverpool, was one of the later lines to be constructed and was more of a gap filler than a major addition to the rail network.

Not all railway companies prospered and some projected lines never got off the ground. There was also much frantic speculation in railway shares, particularly during the so-called 'Railway Mania' of the 1840s, and a number of companies went bust amidst allegations of widespread fraud. One major figure suspected of financial corruption and shady share dealing at this time was George Hudson, nicknamed the Railway King. He had built up a huge railway empire, mainly in Yorkshire and the north-east, but was sent for trial, convicted of fraud and subsequently spent time in prison.

The effects of the railways were tremendous, varied and far-reaching. They created thousands of new jobs, considerably extended the iron and steel and engineering industries and speeded up the movement of goods and raw materials. Agriculture was one of the main beneficiaries as with perishable goods speed was essential and food could now be quickly transported to its markets, especially in the nearby urban and industrial areas. At the same time competition from the railways inevitably caused the decline of the canals and stagecoaches.

New towns sprang up at important railway junctions and centres, such as Crewe and Swindon, and many older towns – York, Derby, Doncaster and Exeter – expanded because of the railways. Suburban expansion gathered pace, especially in London, as people no longer had to live close to their places of work but could commute. One group of towns virtually created by the railways were the large seaside resorts. Lines linked them with nearby urban areas and gave industrial workers a chance to escape from their often grimy and unhealthy surroundings and breathe fresh air at the new seaside resorts of Blackpool, Southend, Margate and Scarborough.

The Wirral Way near Ness

Railways also helped to unify the nation. They made it possible to have a national press instead of just local newspapers, and institutions that were previously organised on a local or regional basis because of slow transport and communications – such as political parties and trade unions – could now operate nationally. All in all the railways brought about a major economic and social revolution in Victorian Britain and continued to have a virtual monopoly of long-distance travel until the advent of motor transport in the early 20th century.

THE WALK

The Wirral Country Park is unique in that it is based almost entirely on a former railway line and hardly extends beyond the width of the track. After it was closed down, the line was converted into the Wirral Way, a 12-mile-long footpath and bridleway that extends along the whole length of the line, apart from two short breaks where building took place before the Country Park and footpath were created.

The railway, which opened in 1865, originally ran along the western side of the Wirral peninsula between Hooton and Parkgate. Later in 1896 it was extended northwards to West Kirby. It provided a link between Chester and Liverpool and carried both goods and passengers. Farm produce and coal were taken to Merseyside and people from Liverpool and other nearby industrial towns were brought to Parkgate and the other seaside resorts on the Wirral. The railway also helped to bring about the development of the Wirral into a commuter area for Liverpool. The decline of traffic after the Second World War led to its inevitable closure. Passenger transport ceased in 1956 and the line finally closed in 1962.

Starting from Hadlow Road station is like stepping back in time to the heyday of steam trains. It has been preserved as it was in 1952 with its original waiting room, ticket office and signal box.

❶ Begin by going on to the station platform and turn right. Go through a gate onto a road, cross over and keep ahead along a most attractive, tree-lined stretch of the Wirral Way. After ½ mile turn left down steps at a waymarked post, go through a kissing gate and turn right along the right edge of a field. Just before reaching a telegraph pole, bear left to continue across the field and climb a stile on the far side. Walk along an enclosed path to the A540.

❷ Cross carefully at the traffic lights and keep ahead along Mill Lane. On the edge of Ness, turn sharp left along Flashes Lane, which becomes a rough track, and at a public footpath sign, turn right along an enclosed path to a tarmac track. Turn right to a road and the Ness Botanic Gardens are just to the left.

Ness Botanic Gardens are situated near the banks of the river Dee overlooking the hills of north Wales. They were begun by Arthur Kilpin Bulley in 1898, an enthusiastic collector of plants and seeds, who sponsored plant hunters to bring back plants from many parts of the world, especially the Far East and Middle East, that could be cultivated in the Wirral soil and climate. After a period of neglect during the Second World War, the gardens were bequeathed to Liverpool University in 1948.

Their attractive and colourful displays, especially of rhododendrons and azaleas, the landscaped terraces, rock garden and water garden delight the many visitors. The gardens are also renowned for their work in horticultural research, education and conservation. As well as a coffee shop, there is a gift shop, lecture theatre and conservatory. Tel: 0151 353 0123.

> **REFRESHMENTS**
>
> There is a pub at Ness and coffee shop at Ness Botanic Gardens. The Four Seasons Coffee Shop serves a selection of snacks and lunches, including quiches, pies, sandwiches, jacket potatoes, homemade soups and cakes, in a most attractive environment. In fine weather you can sit outside at picnic tables. Tel: 0151 353 0123

❸ The route continues to the right into Ness. At a crossroads keep ahead, passing to the right of the Wheatsheaf, and where the road bends left, turn right along an enclosed tarmac track called Cumbers Lane. Keep ahead along an enclosed path, go up three steps into a field and continue along a path which veers left across it to a stile on the far side. Climb it, walk along the left edge of a children's play area to a road and turn right to continue along a tree-lined track. At a yellow-waymarked post turn left along an enclosed path to a track.

❹ Turn right along it, follow the track around a left bend and continue to a disused railway bridge. In front of the bridge, turn left over a stile, climb steps up to a track and turn right over the bridge, here rejoining the Wirral Way. Follow it back to Hadlow Road station, a distance of about 1¼ miles.

WALK 12

ANDERTON BOAT LIFT AND VICTORIAN ENGINEERING

Length: 3 miles

Anderton boat lift

HOW TO GET THERE:
Anderton Nature Park is just off the minor road that runs through Anderton village to the north of Northwich; follow Anderton Boat Lift signs from the A533 and other main roads near Northwich.

PARKING: Pay and display car park at Anderton Nature Park

MAP: OS Explorer 267 (Northwich & Delamere Forest) GR 648754

INTRODUCTION

From the Anderton Boat Lift a pleasant stretch beside the Trent and Mersey Canal leads into the glorious woodland and grassland of Marbury Country Park. From here you enjoy superb views across Budworth Mere to the tower of Great

Budworth church. More delightful and undulating woodland brings you back to the start.

HISTORICAL BACKGROUND

The 19th century is noted for a number of British engineering triumphs and the skills of British engineers were among the primary reasons for the country's economic supremacy for much of the Victorian era. An interesting observation is that the major engineers – civil and mechanical – were largely self-made and self-taught men who achieved their successes by responding to challenges and demands and finding practical solutions to problems without any real education and sometimes with no previous experience. There were virtually no qualifications in engineering or engineering courses at universities and colleges, and the professional organisations – the Institution of Civil Engineers (1818) and Institution of Mechanical Engineers (1847) – provided little in the way of formal training.

It was the tremendous growth in the British economy between the end of the Napoleonic Wars in 1815 and the emergence of German and American

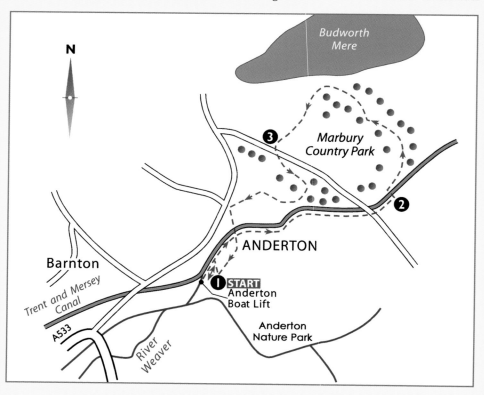

competition after 1870 that created an insatiable demand for engineers and engineering works. The expansion of the coal and iron industries and increased demands for more manufactured goods of all kinds, greater agricultural production and for faster and more efficient transport, created an urgent need for bigger and better machines, more machine parts and huge new projects such as canals, railways, docks, bridges, aqueducts, viaducts, railway stations and factories.

Numerous examples of self-taught engineers can be given. George Stephenson, the pioneer of the railways, was born in a humble cottage, the son of a colliery foreman, and gained his engineering experience in the coal mines of the north-east. His son Robert went on to build some of the finest railway bridges in the country – over the Tyne at Newcastle and the Tweed at Berwick and across the Menai Strait linking Anglesey with the mainland of north Wales. For James Nasmyth, the inventor of the steam hammer and son of an Edinburgh landscape painter, mechanics was a hobby. At least Isambard Kingdom Brunel, responsible for – among many other projects – the Great Western Railway, the earliest steamships and the first tunnel under the Thames, was the son of an engineer but he was still self-taught. And William Armstrong, a multi-talented genius who built hydraulic machinery of all kinds, cranes and engines, bridges and ships, was originally destined for a career in law.

Fortunately many of the great civil engineering projects of the Victorian era have survived and are still in use. Some of the experience needed for these, especially the building of the railway network, was initially acquired from the earlier work of the great canal engineers of the 18th and early 19th centuries – notably Brindley, Smeaton and Telford. The canals were in decline for most of the Victorian period but there were still some spectacular successes. The major project was the Manchester Ship Canal, opened in 1894, but one of the most inventive and unusual examples of Victorian engineering skills was the Anderton Boat Lift, constructed in the early 1870s.

THE WALK

1 Start by walking down to the canal towpath, following a footpath sign to the Boat Lift which is just to the left.

By the 18th century the area around Northwich was a flourishing centre of the salt mining industry and most of the salt was transported along the river Weaver, which also served the pottery industries of north Staffordshire. After 1777 the river was supplemented by the Trent and Mersey Canal. The two waterway companies decided to cooperate rather than compete and where river and canal ran closest to each other at Anderton, a basin was excavated on one bank of the Weaver below the canal in 1793. The problem was how to transfer cargo up and down the 50 ft high embankment that separated them. Initially several methods were tried – using chutes down which to slide

The Trent and Mersey Canal skirts Marbury Country Park

the produce, hoisting it up by cranes – but these were both clumsy and time-consuming. It would be easier if the boats themselves could be transported between river and canal but the building of locks was not a feasible proposition. In the early 1870s the recommended solution was for a boat lift.

It was constructed between 1872 and 1875 and even by the standards of Victorian Britain, the Anderton Boat Lift was a remarkable and fascinating piece of engineering. There were two water-filled containers called caissons which counter-balanced each other. Boats sailed into these caissons which lifted them up and down the incline by hydraulic power. In the early years there were problems with the huge hydraulic rams that were used, mainly leakages of water and corrosion, and because of this the whole system was converted from hydraulic to electrical power in 1908.

This was successful and the boat lift worked well for over half a century but in the 1950s and 60s when usage of the canal declined, it became increasingly difficult to afford the maintenance costs required to keep it open. The discovery of extensive corrosion in the 1980s finally led to its closure. After lying neglected and derelict for a number of years, it was restored by British Waterways in 2002 and given a new lease of life as a tourist attraction and for leisure use. The boat lift is also the focal point of the Anderton Nature Park, one of many recreational areas of woods and meadows in the Northwich area reclaimed from industrial dereliction. Tel: 01606 786777.

The route is to the right along the towpath, following signs to Marbury Country Park and passing Anderton Marina. After about 1 mile – and soon after passing under a road bridge – you reach a footbridge over the canal.

REFRESHMENTS

The café at the Anderton Boat Lift Exhibition Centre serves soup, sandwiches, jacket potatoes, light lunches and soft drinks. As an added bonus it has grand views of the boat lift. Tel: 01606 786777

❷ Go under it, turn right through a fence gap, turn right again and cross the bridge. Keep in the same direction along the other bank of the canal but the path soon bends left into Big Wood, one of the areas of woodland that are either within or on the edge of Marbury Country Park. Following signs to 'Mere', take the right-hand path at a fork, continue along the left-hand path at the next fork, with a stream (Forge Brook) below on the right, and at a T-junction turn right. Soon come great views to the right across Budworth Mere to the tower of Great Budworth church on the hill behind.

Marbury Country Park occupies the grounds of the now vanished Marbury Hall, the former home of the Marbury family who were involved in the development of the salt industry in the locality. The house was demolished in 1969 and the country park was created in 1975. It is renowned for the views across Budworth Mere and its fine woodlands and lime avenues, the latter a legacy from the days when it was a great landed estate.

Continue roughly parallel to the lakeshore before curving left away from the mere to a crossways. Keep ahead, curving left and then bearing right, and continue across open grassland to a footpath post by a junction of paths. Keep ahead, in the Hopyards Wood direction, and go through a gate onto a lane.

❸ Cross over and continue along the winding, undulating path ahead through Hopyards Wood, descending steps and keeping above Marbury Brook to a footbridge.

Turn right over the bridge and the path zigzags up the wooded slopes and continues across a grassy area to a T-junction. Turn left onto another winding path and just before emerging onto a road, take the left-hand path at a fork. Pass beside a barrier into the marina car park and keep ahead to a lane. Turn left, following signs to 'Anderton Boat Lift', and the lane leads back to the start.

WALK 13
LYME PARK AND THE ENGLISH COUNTRY HOUSE

Length: 6 miles

The façade of Lyme Park

HOW TO GET THERE: Disley is on the A6 between Stockport and Chapel-en-le-Frith.

PARKING: Free parking at the railway station car park in Disley

MAP: Explorer OL1 (The Peak District – Dark Peak area) GR 974846

INTRODUCTION

From Disley you soon get out into the glorious, open and rugged countryside of the Peak District and the first part of the route is a more or less continuous ascent, on tracks and paths mostly over rough grassland to the Bow Stones, the highest point on the route. Here you enter Lyme Park, a medieval deer park, and drop down across moorland and through woodland to the great house. The last leg continues across the park back to Disley. The views are both extensive and varied throughout, ranging from the open moorlands of the Peak District and the steep hillsides of the park to the built up area of Greater Manchester.

HISTORICAL BACKGROUND

Although containing earlier work from the Elizabethan period, Lyme Park is basically a grand 18th-century mansion with 19th-century additions and amendments. Therefore its building dates coincide almost exactly with the heyday of the English country house. With its rolling acres and rich farmland, Cheshire possessed many such grand houses surrounded by large estates, including Dunham Massey, Tatton (see walk 6), Adlington and Capesthorne.

It was the period from the end of the 17th century to the outbreak of the First World War that was the great age of the English country houses and their aristocratic owners and occupants. Throughout most of this period the landed

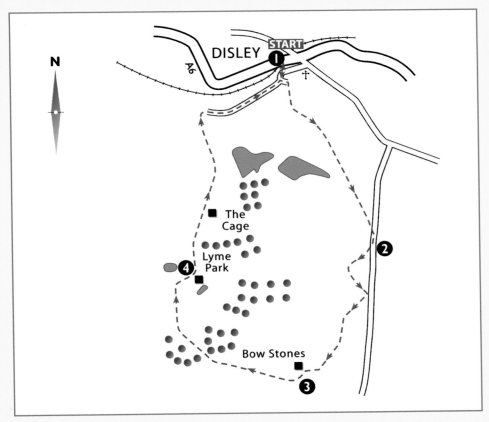

aristocracy dominated the country. The civil wars and rebellions of the 17th century had stripped the monarchy of its absolute power – one king had been executed and another deposed – Parliament was now supreme over the monarchy and the aristocracy controlled Parliament and the government. There might have been two rival political parties in the Houses of Parliament – Whigs and Tories – but both were run by a handful of powerful aristocratic families. It is no accident that until the middle years of the 19th century, all British prime ministers came from the ranks of the landed aristocracy.

The aristocracy were also immensely rich. Between them they owned most of the country, trade was expanding, rents were increasing and the unprecedented growth of population at the time caused an increased demand for food. Some members of the aristocracy, particularly those with estates in the midlands and north, became even wealthier with the advent of the Industrial Revolution as they owned the land on which there were coal deposits and other minerals.

After the upheavals of the previous century, the 18th century was a more settled and peaceful period, free from internal upheaval, save for the brief and unsuccessful Jacobite rebellions which hardly touched the mass of English people. The tenant farmers and farm labourers were generally subservient and too scattered and disorganised to get together in trade unions or mount any resistance against their landlords to improve their lot. Even when internal disturbances surfaced again among the new industrial workers in the 19th century, the main targets for their action were the mill and factory owners not the landed aristocracy.

Therefore, freed from royal power from above and internal strife from below and with ever increasing wealth, the great landowners could spend lavish amounts of money on enlarging and improving their country houses and estates, employing the best architects and landscape gardeners and filling their homes with works of art. Many of these art treasures were accumulated on their Grand Tours of Europe to the leading artistic centres of France and Italy.

Although this power, wealth and idyllic lifestyle could not last forever, the decline of the English country houses and their owners was a gradual one. It began around the middle years of the 19th century. The gradual extension of the right to vote, which started in 1832 and was virtually completed by 1918, shifted the balance of power in Parliament from landowners to industrialists and businessmen, and ultimately to working people. Prime Ministers, beginning with Peel and Gladstone, were now starting to come from the ranks of the northern middle-class industrialists, although as late as 1902 Lord Salisbury sat in the House of Lords while head of government. The House of Lords itself, always dominated by the landowners regardless of who was in power in the Commons, lost its right to veto legislation following the Parliament Act of 1911 and now became the poor relation to the elected House of Commons.

Two major financial factors that contributed to the decline of the great country

The Cage, Lyme Park

houses were the imposition of death duties, first introduced in 1894, and the raising of income tax rates. This weakened the financial base of the landowners and made it difficult for them to afford the maintenance of the grand houses and large estates. The two world wars of the 20th century worsened the situation. In particular during the Second World War many country houses were requisitioned by the army and by 1945 were in a generally bad shape, through a combination of six years of neglect and in some cases bad treatment. Some country houses had already been sold or demolished before the war but the pace quickened in the post-war era.

One solution to the problem of how to maintain these buildings and preserve them for posterity was to open them and their adjoining gardens and parklands to the public as tourist attractions. Sometimes the landowners did this themselves but an alternative was to entrust the job to the National Trust. This is what happened to Lyme Park, now a popular country park where the grounds and house, with their combination of artistic treasures, floral attractions and recreational amenities, can these days be enjoyed and appreciated by all.

THE WALK

❶   The bottom of a flight of steps at the far end of the car park is the start of the Gritstone Trail and much of the walk is on this well-waymarked route. Climb the steps, at the top keep ahead along a lane and take the first turning on the left, signposted to St Mary's church. Walk along a tarmac track which bears right and soon come views of the Peak District moorlands ahead. The tall isolated building seen to the right is The Cage in Lyme Park, passed towards the end of the walk.

At a fingerpost, continue along what is now a rough enclosed track which later narrows to a path. After going through a gate, keep ahead through an area of shrubs and trees, go through another gate and continue along an enclosed track, here leaving the Gritstone Trail. Climb some steps, go through a kissing gate and head gently uphill across rough grassland. Go through another kissing gate onto a road and turn right.

❷   At a footpath post, bear slightly right through a gate and walk along a track across rough grassland to a stile in front of a small group of trees. Do not climb it but turn left and head uphill by a fence on the right. In front of a barn, bear left to go through a gate, walk through a farmyard and the track curves left and continues to a road. Turn sharp right, not along the road but along a lane – there is a public footpath sign to Bow Stones – and continue steadily uphill to reach a public footpath sign and junction of tracks at the top.

The Bow Stones comprise parts of two Anglo-Saxon crosses, possibly placed here sometime in the 16th century as boundary markers. They are at the highest point on the walk, at around 1300 ft, and the views from here over the hills and empty moorlands of the Peak District are magnificent, including, in the distance, the distinctive shape of Shutlingsloe, the 'Cheshire Matterhorn'.

3 Turn right over a stile – to rejoin the main Gritstone Trail – and keep ahead to a ladder stile which admits you to Lyme Park. Follow a path across open moorland which descends to the edge of the trees seen ahead. Go through a gate and as you walk through Knightslow Wood, there are dramatic views to the right of Lyme Hall and The Cage. Go through a gate on the far side of the wood and continue downhill along the left edge of trees to a kissing gate.

Go through and keep ahead along a tarmac track by the left edge of a car park. If you want to visit the coffee shop, turn left beside a small pool but otherwise turn right by an information

The Bow Stones

and refreshment kiosk and go up steps beside the wall bordering the gardens to the entrance to the house.

In 1346 Lyme Park was enclosed as a deer park from the surrounding wilderness of Macclesfield Forest and it is still a deer park today. It was given to the Legh family in 1398 by Richard II as a reward for military valour in the Hundred Years' War with France. The house and estate remained in their possession for nearly 600 years until difficulties with its upkeep caused Richard Legh, 3rd Lord Newton, to give it to the National Trust in 1946.

Around the middle of the 16th century, Sir Piers Legh built a grand Elizabethan mansion on the site of the original small medieval manor house. Substantial parts of this house survive, notably much of the north front, the long gallery – which has some fine Elizabethan panelling – and the drawing room. Major extensions and alterations took place in the 1720s and 30s when the house was transformed into an Italian-style palace by the Venetian architect Giacomo Leoni. He built the most striking feature of the exterior – the elegant and much photographed south front. After a period of neglect, when the house fell into a bad state, it was restored by Lewis Wyatt in the early 19th century. He redesigned most of the interior and added the tower above the south front.

The state rooms contain a wealth of fine paintings, furnishings, wood carvings and tapestries amassed by the Legh family, plus a large collection of clocks. Adjoining the house is the orangery and visitors can wander around the delightful 19th-century formal gardens. Tel: 01663 762023.

④ At the entrance to the house, turn left along a tarmac drive which curves right and at a junction of tracks, turn sharp left onto a worn grassy track. Head gently uphill along a ridge to The Cage, the building seen from near the start of the walk.

> **REFRESHMENTS**
>
> Pubs at Disley and the restaurant and coffee shop at Lyme Park. The Ram's Head just by Disley station is a large, handsome, rambling and cosy pub built around 1840 in the Tudor style. It offers a good range of both light and full lunches and in fine weather the secluded garden is an attractive spot in which to relax over food and a drink. Tel: 01663 767909. The coffee shop in Lyme Park, about two-thirds of the way round the walk, is an equally good place to stop for morning coffee, lunch or afternoon tea. Tel: 01663 762023

Standing on top of the ridge, The Cage is one of the most prominent landmarks in the park. Originally built in Elizabethan times as a viewing platform for the hunt, it was reconstructed in the 18th century.

Continue past The Cage, descending gently, bear slightly right on joining another track and continue down to a tarmac drive. Turn right and at a crossways by the pay kiosk, turn right towards a lodge and go through a gate. Continue gently uphill along a tree-lined lane to a T-junction and turn left. Here you rejoin the outward route and retrace your steps down the wooded bank to Disley station.

WALK 14

PORT SUNLIGHT AND A VICTORIAN PHILANTHROPIST

Length: 1½ miles

The Lady Lever Art Gallery at Port Sunlight

HOW TO GET THERE: Port Sunlight is about 3 miles south of Birkenhead; follow signs from the A41.	**PARKING:** In front of the Lady Lever Art Gallery at Port Sunlight	**MAP:** OS Explorer 266 (Wirral & Chester) GR 337848

INTRODUCTION

Most people have heard of Sunlight Soap. Port Sunlight, where it is manufactured, is one of Britain's pioneering model industrial communities, conceived by one man for his workforce. A walk around its main sites, although short, is a most fascinating and rewarding experience and the moment you turn off the busy main road into the village is like entering another world and a different era. If your interest in such places is whetted by this walk, there is a smaller and earlier version of Port Sunlight just across the other side of the A41 at Bromborough Pool.

HISTORICAL BACKGROUND

Even by Victorian standards William Hesketh Lever was a remarkable man. Born in Bolton in 1851, he began his career as a successful businessman and manufacturer by leasing a small soapworks at Warrington from where he built up a thriving business.

In order to expand, he purchased an area of marshy land on the Wirral near the banks of the river Mersey and here he built a new factory and around it a model village for his workers. He was one of a small group of enlightened employers who was appalled by the squalor and disease prevalent throughout Britain's industrial areas at the time and firmly believed that a healthy and contented workforce would be a more efficient workforce, hence good for business. This was the philosophy behind the creation of Port Sunlight.

The building of the factory and model village began in 1888 and it was heavily influenced by the current garden cities and garden suburbs movement. It was planned on green and spacious lines and all the houses had gardens and were far in advance of most working-class housing in Britain at the time. The idea was to create something on the lines of a traditional English village and in order to achieve this, Lever employed over 30 architects who contributed different styles.

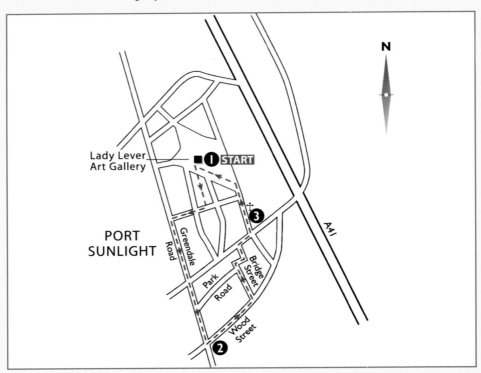

Parkland at Port Sunlight

This means that, unlike smaller estate villages, the buildings are not uniform. Lever, who was closely involved in the development of the village at every stage, was interested in healthy minds as well as healthy bodies. He built schools, institutes and swimming pools and encouraged people to improve their education and engage in healthy outdoor and sporting activities. Clubs and societies were set up and he was particularly keen on his workers growing their own food on allotments.

In many ways Lever was a man of contradictions. He was paternalistic, liked to get his own way and laid down elaborate rules and regulations but at the same time he was generous and prepared to be flexible. An outstanding example of this latter quality is that although a strict teetotaller, he allowed the temperance hotel he built – now the Bridge Inn – to sell alcohol when a majority of the workers indicated their preference for this.

In recognition of his outstanding achievements, he was created Lord Leverhulme in 1917. He died in 1925 and nowadays the village that he created is maintained by a Village Trust.

THE WALK

Lever and his wife were a devoted couple and he attributed much of his success to her. He was devastated by her death in 1913 and almost immediately began the construction of the Lady Lever Art Gallery in her memory. It was opened in 1922 and houses a fine collection of paintings, furniture, sculpture and tapestries. Tel: 0151 478 4136. Just around the corner is the Leverhulme Memorial, unveiled in 1930 five years after Lord Leverhulme's death.

Across the road on the corner of King George's Drive is the Sunlight Vision Museum, housed in a building opened in 1913 for use as a club for girls. It tells the story of the development of Port Sunlight from its beginnings in the 1880s to the start of the First World War and a visit here is highly recommended as a prelude to the walk. Tel: 0151 644 6466.

❶ With your back to the art gallery, walk along the tarmac path by a fountain and between flower beds that bisects the broad boulevard lined by King George's Drive on the left and Queen Mary's Drive on the right. On reaching the striking war memorial, turn right beside the Garden Centre on the left, established on the site of an outdoor swimming pool, and at a T-junction, turn left along Greendale Road. At the corner of Park Road you pass the Village Tea Rooms on the left and the station on the right.

> ### REFRESHMENTS
>
> At Port Sunlight there is the Bridge Inn and Village Tea Rooms, plus cafés at the Garden Centre and Lady Lever Art Gallery. The café in the basement of the Art Gallery, conveniently situated at the start of the walk and opposite the Sunlight Vision Museum, has a pleasantly old-fashioned air and provides morning coffee, afternoon tea and a wide selection of cooked and light lunches. Tel: 0151 478 4136

❷ In front of Lever House, the administrative headquarters of Lever's industrial empire opened in 1896, turn left into Wood Street; turn first left into Bridge Street and ahead is the Lyceum.

The Lyceum was built between 1894 and 1896 and originally served as both village school and church. Later it became a staff training college and is now used as a social club.

Cross a footbridge over the attractive sunken gardens of The Dell to the Lyceum and to the left is Bridge Cottage, Lever's temporary home in 1896–97 while his main residence, Thornton Manor, was being renovated. Turn right beside the Lyceum, turn left into Cross Street and at a junction, turn right along Bolton Road, passing in front of Hulme Hall. This was built in 1901–02 as a dining hall for women.

❸ Turn left in front of the Bridge Inn along Church Drive, passing Christ Church.

Both Lord Leverhulme and his wife are buried in Christ Church which was built at his own expense as a gift to the villagers. It was opened in 1904 as a Congregational church and is now a United Reformed church.

Continue along the drive and just after passing the school, turn left along Windy Bank to return to the art gallery.

WALK 15

THURSTASTON AND SECOND WORLD WAR DEFENCES

Length: 6 miles

These bumps in the ground are all that remains of Thurstaston's anti-aircraft defences

HOW TO GET THERE:
Thurstaston Visitor Centre is on the Wirral Way; follow signs to Wirral Country Park from the A540 at Thurstaston village

between West Kirby and Heswall.

PARKING: Wirral Country Park

MAP: OS Explorer 266 (Wirral & Chester) GR 238835

INTRODUCTION

The opening and closing stretches are along the Wirral Way, with fine views across the Dee estuary to north Wales. In between you climb the glorious heathery and gorse-strewn slopes of Thurstaston Hill, a magnificent viewpoint, and walk across fields and through the wooded dell of The Dungeon.

HISTORICAL BACKGROUND

Aerial warfare really began in the First World War and some anti-aircraft defences had been hastily erected as early as 1913, when war with Germany was looking a distinct possibility, to protect key military targets, mainly around London. These targets included coastal batteries, arsenals, munitions factories, dockyards and wireless stations.

Between the end of the First World War and the outbreak of the Second World War, little else was done. Anti-aircraft defences were regarded as a 'Cinderella' area for defence spending and, in view of developments in military aircraft, some politicians were sceptical about their value. In 1931 the Conservative leader Stanley Baldwin stated that 'the bomber will always get through'.

With war impending, something had to be done and in April 1939 Anti-Aircraft Command was set up, led by Sir Frederick Pile. This remarkable and widely respected man remained in charge throughout the war and retired in 1945 a few weeks before the collapse of Nazi Germany. Because of its 'Cinderella' status, he had to fight constantly for funding against intense competition from other branches of the armed forces and other areas of defence needs.

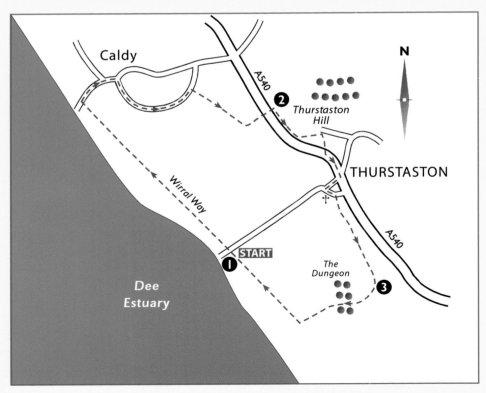

Despite this the provision of anti-aircraft defences expanded rapidly, especially in the early years of the war when the danger from the Luftwaffe was at its greatest. Heavy anti-aircraft sites rose from only 622 at the start of the war in September 1939 – over half of which were around London – to over 1000 by 1942. After that, as the danger from German bombing raids subsided, there was little new provision and many of the sites ceased to be maintained.

After the war they were ignored and neglected because there was little interest in keeping them. With advances in military techniques, they were by now largely redundant and they were too recent and of little architectural or picturesque appeal to be preserved as historic monuments compared to earlier military sites. However, the Second World War is now receding into history and anti-aircraft sites are as much a part of our heritage as Roman forts, medieval castles and later artillery defences erected in the Tudor, Stuart and Victorian eras. They are the only physical representation – however slight – of Britain's wartime air defence system which played such a vital role in frustrating Hitler's ambitions to invade and conquer this country and ensuring our eventual victory.

THE WALK

Liverpool and Merseyside as a whole were prime targets for Hitler's bombers. The city was, from 1941 onwards, the headquarters of the Western Approaches Command – located in Derby House – a major port and the centre of one of Britain's most heavily industrialised areas. Therefore as bombing raids became more frequent and intense, Liverpool and the surrounding area was protected by a ring of heavy anti-aircraft gun sites. Thurstaston was one of these and a gun emplacement was built beside the railway line in order that munitions and other essentials could be transported by train to Thurstaston station.

It has to be said that there is little to see and a great deal of imagination is required to envisage it as it was during the war. The only physical evidence are the slight bumps that can be made out on the grassy cliff top near the visitor centre.

The walk starts by the disused railway line on the site of the former Thurstaston station. For details of the opening times of the Visitor Centre, phone 0151 648 4371 or 3884.

❶ Start by facing the estuary and turn right along the Wirral Way between the remains of the former station platforms. Keep along it for nearly 1½ miles to a road and turn right into the leafy residential area of Caldy.

For details of the Wirral Way see walk 11.

Follow the road around right and left bends to a T-junction and turn right along Croft Drive East. The road curves left and opposite Long Hey Road, turn right, at a public footpath sign to Thurstaston Hill, along an enclosed track.

The Dee estuary at Thurstaston

Follow the track around a left bend, go through a gate and keep ahead to the A540.

2 Cross over, turn right and almost immediately take the enclosed path which runs parallel to the road, heading uphill along the right edge of trees. Bear left, continue up through the trees, cross a path and climb more steeply up through heather and gorse to a sandstone outcrop. Turn right and continue to the view indicator and trig point on the summit of Thurstaston Hill.

Despite its modest height of 299 ft, Thurstaston Hill is a wonderful viewpoint. From here the views extend in all directions: along the length of the Wirral Peninsula, across the Dee estuary to the hills of north Wales and over the other side of the Mersey to the cathedral and other prominent buildings in Liverpool city centre.

The hill and surrounding common, together with the neighbouring Royden Park, comprise around 250 acres of parkland, woodland and heath and provide an invaluable open area and wildlife habitat close to the heavily built up Merseyside conurbation. It was almost lost in the 19th century as in 1879 a group of local landowners tried to enclose the common. Widespread opposition, which was supported by Birkenhead

Council, ensured that the highest and most attractive areas remained as places for public recreation. Subsequent donations of land to the National Trust have added to those areas.

Keep along the main path which descends to a track and turn right. Continue through trees to the A540 again and turn left, passing the Cottage Loaf. At a crossroads just beyond the pub, turn right down Station Road to a T-junction and turn left. Where the road bends left, keep ahead, at a public footpath sign to Heswall, along a track, passing to the left of Thurstaston's 19th-century church. Climb a stile, walk along an enclosed path, go through a kissing gate and continue along the path, climbing a series of stiles, to reach a belt of trees and a footpath post.

❸ Turn right, in the Wirral Way direction, through the trees, cross the brook on the right and continue through the woodland of The Dungeon. At a fork, take the waymarked left-hand path which descends to a T-junction. Turn left, descend steps, recross the brook and turn right to continue along an enclosed path which eventually rises to meet the Wirral Way. Turn right and follow it back to the start.

WALK 16
JODRELL BANK AND MODERN ASTRONOMY

Length: 6½ miles

The Lovell Telescope at Jodrell Bank

HOW TO GET THERE: Jodrell Bank is signposted from the A535 between Holmes Chapel and Alderley Edge.

PARKING: Jodrell Bank Visitor Centre

MAP: OS Explorer 268 (Wilmslow, Macclesfield & Congleton) GR 796713

INTRODUCTION

The walk takes you through the pleasant, flat and well-wooded Cheshire countryside between the M6, Macclesfield, Alderley Edge and Congleton. The main feature of interest is the giant Lovell Telescope at Jodrell Bank which dominates the surrounding landscape and can be seen from several points on the route. It is important to take care on the two short stretches of main road walking near the beginning and end; the A535 is a busy road and there is not much of a verge in places.

HISTORICAL BACKGROUND

From the earliest times man has been fascinated by the stars and the wonders of the universe. All the ancient civilisations – Mesopotamian, Egyptian, Indian, Chinese, Greek and Roman – observed the objects in the sky and had their own theories about their meaning and purpose, usually closely linked with mysticism and their different religious beliefs.

In the Middle Ages it was the Islamic world that was in the forefront of astronomical advance and there were observatories in most of the major cities of the Middle East. European astronomy did not advance much until the Renaissance when a Polish astronomer, Copernicus, first developed the idea that the planets revolved around the sun. Galileo expanded on this and was among the first to make use of a telescope. Later Sir Isaac Newton linked astronomy and physics through his theory of gravity by showing that the gravitational pull of the Earth was the same as that which held the moon in orbit around our planet.

It was 20th-century technology, especially photography, which caused the greatest advances. The universe could now be studied in greater detail and other galaxies could be observed. Astronomy developed at a particularly fast pace after the Second World War as astronomers and scientists tried to increase their understanding of the universe by harnessing some of the technology – such as radar – that had arisen out of the needs of the war.

In Britain the leading pioneer was Bernard Lovell, a lecturer at Manchester University. He had worked on radar systems during the war and returned to the university in 1945 with the aim of furthering his research into cosmic rays, the particles that enter the Earth's atmosphere from outer space. In order to do this he set up a research unit at Jodrell Bank. The first telescopes were not adequate and bigger, more refined – and more expensive – ones were required. Lovell began to investigate radio waves emitted from objects in space, even from those outside our own galaxy, the Milky Way, and in the early 1950s work began on the construction of the giant telescope.

When this telescope was completed in 1957 it was the largest steerable radio telescope in the world. The commencement of its work coincided with the start of the space race as in the same year the Russians launched the Sputnik, the first satellite. This proved to be an unexpected blessing for Lovell and the Jodrell Bank Observatory. The huge cost of the telescope to the taxpayer had provoked a barrage of criticism in Parliament and elsewhere but its use in the tracking of satellites and space missiles on behalf of the United States helped to defray the costs and reduce the debts.

Although satellite tracking helped to pay the bills, the main purpose was research into the universe and its origins and this is what the giant telescope has done. It has been continually refined, upgraded and improved over the last half century and has been instrumental in the discovery of quasars, among the most distant of the luminous objects in the universe. In 1961 Lovell received a knighthood for his outstanding work at Jodrell Bank. Since its completion the

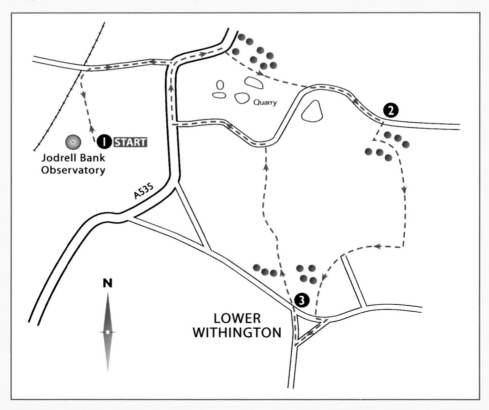

The Lovell Telescope seen from the gardens

Lovell Telescope has been in the forefront of astronomical research and is now at the heart of a network of international radio telescopes.

THE WALK

The giant radio telescope, the first in the world, is the focal point and flagship of the Jodrell Bank Observatory. On its thirtieth birthday in 1987 it was named the Lovell Telescope in honour of its founder. Close up its presence is overpowering and despite its purely functional purpose, it could even be described as an object of beauty.

It arose out of the desire of Bernard Lovell to use his knowledge of radar systems, acquired during the Second World War, to research into cosmic rays. After his return to Manchester University in 1945 he set up his research unit not in the urban surroundings of Manchester but in the University Botanical Gardens at Jodrell Bank, deep in the Cheshire countryside to the south of the city. More powerful telescopes were needed and work on the construction of the giant telescope began in the 1950s. It was completed in 1957.

An Observational Pathway allows you to walk around part of the base of the telescope, where a series of information boards provide detailed and interesting information. The telescope sits on a circular railway track that allows it to move which extends its observational capabilities.

There is more to see than you may think at Jodrell Bank and not all of it is to do with telescopes, the planets and radio waves. As a complete contrast, you can visit the Environmental Discovery Centre and take a relaxing stroll through the Granada Arboretum from which there are striking views of the telescope. To return to the primary astronomical role, you can observe the stars and the solar system in the film theatre at the Visitor Centre where there is also a shop and café. Tel: 01477 571339.

> ### REFRESHMENTS
>
> There is a café at Jodrell Bank Visitor Centre and you pass the Red Lion at Lower Withington, conveniently located at about the half-way point of the walk. The pub serves good home-cooked food both in the bar and restaurant and has an attractive beer garden and plenty of picnic tables outside. The varied menu ranges from full meals to light lunches of soup, jacket potatoes, sandwiches and paninis. Tel: 01477 571248

❶ Make your way back along the drive to the road and turn right. On joining the main road (A535), bear left – be careful, this is a busy road and the verges are not that good – and just after passing the entrance to Dingle Bank Quarry, turn right, at a restricted byway sign, to a gate. Go through and walk along a wooded path which later ascends to continue along the right inside edge of the trees. The quarry is seen over to the right.

Bear left on emerging onto a track, keep along the right inside edge of woodland and at a fork, take the right-hand track. Pass between farm buildings, continue along a tarmac track to a lane and keep ahead.

❷ Where the lane bears slightly left, turn right, at a public footpath sign, along an enclosed track. At a T-junction in front of the gates of a cottage, turn left through a gate and continue through woodland studded with small pools. Keep on the main path all the time, go through a gate and keep ahead to a track at a U-bend. Turn right and the track later becomes enclosed and passes to the left of a cottage. Go through a gate, continue along the enclosed track, go through another gate and keep by a left field edge to a T-junction. Turn right; at a fork keep ahead along the left-hand track, passing to the left of a barn, and follow the track around a left bend to reach the end of a lane.

After curving left in front of a house, immediately turn right along a track that keeps by the right edge of woodland. In front of buildings veer left off the track to a stile, climb it and another one ahead and walk along the left edge of a field. Cross a footbridge in the corner and keep along the left edge of two more fields to emerge onto a road via a stile. Turn left and take the first road on the right to the Red Lion in Lower Withington. At the pub turn sharp right and turn left on rejoining the previous road.

Woodland near Jodrell Bank

❸ At a public footpath sign to Catchpenny Lane, turn right – not along the track but onto a parallel enclosed path to the left of it. After climbing a stile, bear left diagonally across a field to climb another stile in the corner. Keep in the same direction across the next field, climb a stile and continue along a narrow enclosed path. Bear left on emerging onto a track to reach a lane at a U-bend.

Turn right and where the lane ends, keep ahead along a track through woodland. After emerging from the trees, continue along an enclosed track, pass by farm buildings and keep ahead along what is now a tarmac track to a lane. Turn left to the A535, turn right along it – again take care – and where the main road bends right, turn left and retrace your steps to the start.

Other walking guides on the county published by Countryside Books

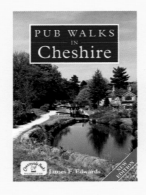

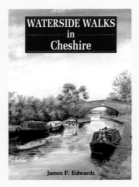

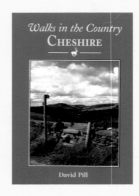